# Bali Travel Guide 2023:

## Bali's Exciting Adventure

**TIMOTHY S. BALDERAS**

# Tablet of contents

## Chapter 14. Sustainable Tourism in Bali

Eco-friendly Practices

Responsible Travel Tips

Supporting Local Communities

## Chapter 15. Beyond Bali

Day Trips from Bali

Nearby Islands and Attractions

# Chapter 1. Introduction to Bali

## *Overview of Bali*

Bali, sometimes referred to as the "Island of the Gods," is a tropical paradise in the Indonesian archipelago. Bali has grown to be a well-liked travel destination for travellers from all over the world because of its magnificent beaches, vibrant culture, stunning surroundings, and welcoming people. Bali offers a fascinating experience that leaves a lasting impression on everyone who visits with its unique combination of spiritual tradition and natural beauty.

One of Bali's most attractive characteristics is the variety of its scenery. With everything from pristine white sand beaches to terraced rice fields and volcanic peaks, the island's natural beauty is breathtaking. Bali has activities to suit everyone's tastes, whether you like to unwind on

Kuta's sun-kissed beaches or explore Ubud's emerald-green rice terraces.

In addition to its natural beauty, Bali has a rich cultural legacy. On the island, there are several temples, where ornate stone sculptures and exciting activities provide a glimpse into the culture. Tourists may immerse themselves in the local arts, dance performances, and rituals that have been performed for generations in Ubud, Bali's spiritual hub.

Bali's thriving wellness industry is ideal for anyone seeking to relax and reenergize. All around the island are opulent spas, yoga retreats, and holistic health centres that provide a wide variety of wellness-related activities. No matter if you wish to indulge in a traditional Balinese massage, practice yoga in a serene setting, or participate in meditation sessions, Bali provides a variety of opportunities to nourish the mind, body, and spirit.

Another draw for visitors to Bali is the local cuisine. The island offers a delectable range of flavours, from high-end restaurants to beautiful street food. Balinese cuisine is known for its unusual blends of sweet, salty, and spicy flavours. Take advantage of the opportunity to try local delicacies like satay, nasi goreng, and babi guling (spit-roasted pig).

Outside of the well-known tourist destinations, Bali offers undiscovered gems that are waiting to be discovered. By deviating from the main path, you may find undiscovered natural splendours, historic villages, and secret beaches. When snorkelling or scuba diving, visit the stunning coral reefs that are filled with marine life to discover the underwater world. Visit the ancient Goa Gajah (Elephant Cave) or the holy water temples of Tirta Empul to discover Bali's esoteric side.

One of Bali's main draws is the kind and welcoming inhabitants. The Balinese are noted for their friendly demeanour, genuine smiles, and sense of community. Interacting with the locals and learning about their culture is a fun experience that can have a lasting effect.

In summary, Bali is an amazing place with attractions for all kinds of visitors. Whether you're seeking leisure, adventure, cultural immersion, or spiritual enlightenment, the island's diverse beauty, rich traditions, and warm hospitality provide a one-of-a-kind experience. With its stunning beaches, lush rice terraces, vibrant arts scene, and mouthwatering cuisine, Bali is a tropical paradise that will make you want to return again.

## Geography and Climate

The topography of Bali is characterised by its diverse landscapes, which range from flawless beaches and lush rice terraces to commanding volcanic highlands and dense rainforests. The island is about 153 kilometres (95 miles) wide and 5,780 kilometres (2,231 miles) in size. Bali is easy to tour due to its tiny size, allowing visitors to get acquainted with its varied surroundings quickly.

One of Bali's most well-known features is its stunning beaches. Due to its miles of sandy coasts and clear waters, the island is a haven for beachgoers, surfers, and beach lovers. From the bustling shorelines of Kuta and Seminyak to the serene and secluded coasts of Nusa Dua and Uluwatu, Bali offers beaches to suit every preference.

In addition to its beaches, Bali is also known for its verdant rice terraces that cascade down the slopes like green steps. The intricate irrigation and farming practices that have maintained Bali's agricultural tradition for millennia are highlighted by the UNESCO-recognized cultural environment of the Subak system. The island's central city of Ubud is an excellent spot to start exploring these spectacular terraces and experiencing traditional Balinese culture.

Geographically speaking, Bali moves into a hilly inner region with volcanic peaks. Of them, Mount Agung, an active volcano with a height of 3,031 metres (9,944 feet), is the most well-known. For the more adventurous traveller, climbing Mount Agung or exploring Mount Batur's caldera offers breathtaking views and an unforgettable experience.

The climate of Bali, which has two distinct seasons—the dry season and the rainy season—is best characterised as tropical weather. The dry season, which typically lasts from April to September, is the most favoured time to visit Bali. The weather at this time of year is defined by a sunny sky, low humidity, and high temperatures, making it perfect for beach vacations and outdoor activities.

The rainy season, which lasts from October to March, is still a great time to go to Bali provided you don't mind the odd downpour. Due to the beautiful foliage and fewer visitors at this season, the island is particularly alluring.

Remember that Bali's weather may be unpredictable and that rain showers can occur, although less often, even during the dry season.

It's important to consider Bali's topography and climate in order to make the most of your trip. Whether tourists are searching for sun-drenched beaches, magnificent landscapes, or to immerse themselves in the vibrant Balinese culture, Bali offers a broad array of attractions that will astonish them. With its appealing landscape and warm atmosphere, Bali certainly lives up to its reputation as a tropical paradise for all sorts of travellers.

## Cultural Background

Indonesia's lovely island of Bali is widely recognized for its vibrant and unique cultural history. It is known for its rich cultural legacy, which is heavily inspired by Hinduism, and attracts tourists from all over the world. Bali offers a captivating experience that showcases the island's unique cultural fabric via its ancient temples, traditional celebrations, and superb arts and crafts.

One aspect of Balinese culture is the people's devotion to Hinduism. In Bali, Hinduism is practised, as opposed to other parts of Indonesia where the majority religion is Islam. The island is covered with thousands of temples, ranging in size from little village shrines to enormous complexes. Since the locals maintain their rituals and ceremonies with a tight sense of religion, visitors have the opportunity to see and get absorbed in the spiritual traditions of the Balinese people.

Bali residents are known for their warm welcome and generosity, which helps tourists feel at home and embraced by the community. The Balinese perform a daily ceremony called "canang sari," which is performed in front of one's home, temple, or place of business as a gift to the gods, in which they weave little baskets from palm leaves and fill them with flowers, rice, and incense. These colourful presents enliven Bali's streets and provide a peaceful, spiritual atmosphere.

Bali's dance and music had a great historical impact on the island. Traditional dances like the Barong dance, Legong, and Kecak are not only visually appealing but also tell stories from Hindu mythology and epics. The rhythmic sounds of the gamelan orchestra, a traditional ensemble made up of metallophones, gongs, and percussion instruments, provide a mesmerising and engrossing experience for tourists while they watch these dances.

There is a ton of art and craftsmanship in Bali, and various artistic expressions may be seen everywhere. The intricate wood carvings, stone sculptures, and paintings depict Balinese and Hindu mythological scenes. The artistic hub of Bali, Ubud, is renowned for its galleries and studios where visitors may see artists at work and even try their hand at creating unique pieces of art. Bali's artistic past may be seen in the batik clothes, silver jewellery, and traditional weaving, all of which provide visitors a range of unique treasures to take home.

It is highly recommended to attend Bali's vibrant festivals and ceremonies. The most well-known of these is Nyepi, commonly referred to as the Day of Silence, which honours the Balinese New Year. There are no lights, no noises, and no activities on the whole island on this day. Visitors may get a sense of the profundity of Balinese spirituality during this time of reflection, fasting, and meditation.

Finally, tourists may profit from and take pleasure in Bali's rich cultural legacy. The island's devotion to Hinduism, warm hospitality, traditional dances, vibrant arts, and spectacular festivals all contribute to its distinctive allure. By exploring Bali's cultural past, one may enter a world where spirituality and artistic expression coexist, leaving a lasting impression on those who are fortunate enough to visit this seductive island.

# Chapter 2. Planning Your Trip

## *Best Time to Visit Bali*

In Bali, visitors could enjoy a unique experience. Choosing the appropriate time to visit Bali may significantly enhance your trip, even if the weather and other festivals may have a significant impact. In this piece, we'll examine the various occasions and times of year to assist you in deciding when to plan your Bali holiday.

On the island of Bali, there are two distinct seasons: the dry season and the rainy season. The dry season, which lasts from April to September, is often believed to be the best time to visit Bali. The weather is sunny the whole time, the humidity is relatively low, and there isn't much rain. The island's warm to hot climate makes it ideal for beach activities, water sports, and exploring its cultural and natural assets. Since Bali's world-class waves are at their best during the dry season, surfers like it more than other seasons.

On the other hand, Bali's rainy season, which lasts from October to March, is characterised by increased rainfall and humidity. While the rainy season may discourage some people from going, it is also beautiful and offers advantages. When the rivers and waterfalls are flowing at their maximum, the surrounding lush greenery shines even more brilliantly. Additionally, the wet season is regarded as the off-season, which means fewer tourists and lower hotel costs. If you don't mind the occasional downpours and want to learn about Bali's rich cultural past, splash out on spa treatments, or enjoy some quiet time in nature, the rainy season can be a great option.

Another consideration while planning your trip to Bali is the calendar of local celebrations and activities. Bali is well known for its vibrant religious celebrations and ceremonies that provide a wonderful window into the way of life of the locals. One of the most significant events is the "Day of Silence," or Nyepi, which occurs in March or April. On Nyepi, the whole island is black, and the locals observe a day of fasting, meditation, and solitude. It is an extraordinary experience to see Bali in complete darkness, with no lights, noise, or outside activity taking place.

If you want to find out more about Bali's artistic and cultural history, you must go to the Ubud Writers and Readers Festival, which is held in October. Literary discussions, seminars, and performances with well-known writers, poets, and artists from across the world are held during the festival. It's a fantastic opportunity to engage with the local and international artistic community while admiring the beautiful town of Ubud.

According to the Balinese calendar, the Galungan festival, which occurs every 210 days, is another significant religious holiday that is fervently celebrated all across the island.

Balinese people execute elaborate ceremonies, decorate bamboo poles, and offer traditional sacrifices to honour Galungan, a period when they believe the ghosts of their ancestors descend to earth. This festival offers a glimpse into the very religious and spiritual Balinese people.

The best time for travellers to go to Bali depends on their priorities, which may include the weather, crowd levels, or experiencing the island's vibrant festivals. The dry season, which lasts from April to September, is sometimes considered as the busiest travel time due to its bright weather and little rainfall. Due to the beautiful environment, lower pricing, and less visitors, the rainy season, which lasts from October to March, may also be a fantastic time to visit. By taking part in occasions like Galungan, the Ubud Writers and Readers Festival, and Nyepi, you may further ingratiate yourself with Bali culture. In the end, Bali's beauty and allure are waiting for you throughout the year, so choose the season that best matches your travel preferences and begin making plans for an unforgettable journey to this mysterious island.

If you're a serious surfer, the best time to go to Bali would be during the dry season, particularly between May and September. Popular surfing spots like Uluwatu, Padang Padang, and Canggu provide consistent waves and favourable wave conditions throughout this season. Famous surf sites in Bali welcome surfers of all levels, from beginners to specialists, and provide an exhilarating experience for wave enthusiasts.

For those seeking a balance between outdoor activities and cultural exploration, the months of April, May, June, and September are ideal. You may benefit from the good weather, minimal crowds, and affordable prices during this shoulder season. It's the perfect time to see Bali's diverse landscapes, wander through lush forests to hidden waterfalls, and completely immerse yourself in local traditions without the throngs of high season.

If you're curious about the underwater world and eager to view Bali's magnificent coral reefs, the dry season is once again the best time to go there. The island's surrounding waters are crystal clear and provide exceptional visibility for diving and snorkelling. Since the ocean currents bring nutrient-rich waters that are home to a variety of marine animals, including manta rays and sunfish (Mola-Mola), divers will especially enjoy the months of May through July.

It's crucial to keep in mind that certain areas, particularly the southern tourist destinations of Kuta, Seminyak, and Ubud, may get crowded even during the dry season owing to Bali's popularity as a tourism destination. If you prefer a more serene and private experience, think about going to one of Bali's less popular regions, such the eastern coast, the northern highlands of Munduk and Bedugul, or the calm beaches of Amed and Nusa Dua.

Finally, it's crucial to keep in mind that Bali's tropical climate might deliver unexpected showers even during the dry season. A lightweight rain jacket or umbrella is a need to have on hand in case of sudden downpours. However, as these downpours often stop quickly, you are free to keep travelling and enjoy Bali's breathtaking natural beauty.

In conclusion, Bali is enticing year-round and provides a broad range of activities that transcend the passing of the seasons. The best time for travellers to visit Bali ultimately depends on what they want, whether they desire wonderful weather, little people, or the chance to participate in regional festivities. Bali's attraction never fades, inviting travellers to enjoy an extraordinary vacation to this tropical paradise with its lush landscapes during the rainy season and its sun-drenched beaches during the dry season.

# *Visa Requirements*

If you're considering travelling to Bali, it's essential to understand the visa requirements in order to ensure a straightforward and hassle-free journey. We'll speak about how travellers to Bali must get a visa.

Visa Exemptions:

Many countries are eligible for visa-free entry to Bali. These countries include a number of others as well as the United States, Canada, the United Kingdom, Australia, and most of the EU members. These tourists may enter Bali and stay there for up to 30 days without getting a visa. It's crucial to keep in mind that this time limit cannot be extended; thus, if you wish to stay for a longer period of time, you must apply for a visa beforehand.

Visa on Arrival (VoA):

Visitors from countries that do not qualify for visa exemption may enter Indonesia using a Visa on Arrival (VoA). This visa, which allows you to stay in Bali for up to 30 days, may be obtained upon arrival at the Ngurah Rai International Airport or other recognized ports of entry. Payment for the VoA is required in cash and may be made in either US dollars or Indonesian rupiah. Since the current VoA pricing is liable to vary, it is advisable that you check the most recent information before your trip.

Social and Cultural Visa:

If you want to stay in Bali longer than 30 days, you must apply for a Social-Cultural Visa, also known as the B-211 Visa, before arriving. You are allowed to stay in Indonesia with this visa for up to 60 days, with the possibility of an additional 30 days once you arrive. To get a social-cultural visa, you must get in touch with the Indonesian embassy or consulate in your nation and provide the necessary documentation, including a letter of sponsorship from an Indonesian individual or group.

Single-Entry Permit:

If you often go to Bali or Indonesia, think about obtaining a multiple entry visa. With this visa, you are allowed to enter and exit the country several times over the course of a year. It will be especially useful for business travellers and those who often go to adjacent countries and wish to return to Bali. Because the Multiple Entry Visa requires a more complicated application process, including sponsorship and supporting papers, see the Indonesian embassy or consulate for the exact requirements.

Extended Stay:

If you are already in Bali and want to stay longer than is permitted, you may do so by submitting an application for a visa extension at the local immigration office. The steps for obtaining an extension involve supplying the appropriate papers, paying the associated fees, and completing the required forms. Extensions are often given for an additional 30 days. You should begin the extension process before your current visa expires in order to avoid any legal difficulties.

In conclusion, visitors to Bali must be informed of the visa requirements for a hassle-free trip. Regardless of whether you qualify for visa exemption, wish to get a Visa on Arrival, or are considering a Social-Cultural or Multiple Entry Visa, it's crucial to familiarise yourself with the necessary paperwork and procedures. By following the visa regulations and being informed of any changes, you can enjoy your time in Bali, taking in its natural beauty and immersing yourself in its rich culture, without worrying about your legal situation.

## *Health and Safety Tips*

Prioritising your health and safety is essential while visiting this tropical paradise. By following these health and safety advice, you may ensure a pleasant and trouble-free trip to Bali.

1. Keep Hydrated: Due to Bali's tropical climate, which can become rather hot and steamy, it's crucial to keep hydrated. Drink plenty of bottled water throughout the day to avoid being dehydrated, especially if you're exercising or spending time outdoors.

2. Wear sunscreen: Bali's sun may be severe, so apply sunscreen with a high SPF before venturing outdoors to protect your skin from UV radiation. Remember to wear a hat, sunglasses,

and light, breathable clothing to avoid overexposure to the sun.

3. Eat Safely: Despite the fact that Bali is renowned for its delectable local cuisine, it's important to be mindful of food safety. You should only go to reputable institutions that maintain acceptable hygiene standards. Avoid eating raw or undercooked food and pick fruits that can be peeled to reduce the risk of illness.

4. Be Aware of Your Environment: Even though it's generally safe to go to Bali, it's always a good idea to exercise caution and be aware of your surroundings. Keep an eye on your belongings, especially in crowded areas, and store valuables in hotel safes or lockers that you can lock. Take care while taking a solitary walk at night, in low-light conditions, or in an unknown area.

5. Swim Safely: Bali's stunning beaches tempt tourists to go swimming, but caution is advised. Swim only in designated areas where lifeguards

are present, and watch out for coral reefs, other potential hazards, and strong currents. If you don't feel at ease in the water, consider wearing a life jacket or receiving professional assistance.

6. Vaccinate yourself: Before travelling to Bali, ask a medical professional about the recommended vaccines. Keep your regular vaccines up to date and consider receiving additional doses, such as those for Hepatitis A and Typhoid, since the risk of exposure may vary depending on your activities and length of stay.

7. Avoid Getting Bites by Mosquitoes: Bali is a tropical location where mosquito bites are possible, particularly during the rainy season. To protect yourself, put on long sleeves and pants and use insect repellent containing DEET or other potent chemicals. Consider using mosquito netting to sleep, especially while staying in open-air accommodations.

8. Practise ethical wildlife tourism: Bali offers opportunities for tourists to interact closely with animals like elephants, monkeys, and sea turtles. But be sure that these interactions are conducted ethically and sensibly. Don't support businesses that mistreat animals or exploit them for entertainment.

9. Travel Insurance: It's usually a good idea to have enough travel insurance while visiting any area. Make sure your insurance covers medical expenses, emergency evacuation, and trip cancellation or delay. Read the fine print to make sure that risky pastimes or water activities are covered.

By following these safety and health advice, you may make the most of your trip to Bali while maintaining your health. Respect local traditions and customs, look after the environment, and take advantage of the numerous cultural opportunities that this beautiful island offers.

## *Transportation Options*

Transportation is one of the most important things to think about while planning a trip to Bali. Fortunately, the island offers a variety of transportation options to meet the needs and preferences of various travellers. Whether you're looking for comfort, affordability, or a spice of adventure, Bali can meet your demands.

1. Taxis: Taxis are a common mode of transportation in Bali, particularly in urban areas like Denpasar and Kuta. There are many metered taxis and ride-hailing services like Grab. Taxis are a convenient choice for quick trips, airport transfers, and hauling heavy loads of luggage. Verify that the driver has set a cost or is utilising the metre before the journey starts.

2. Ride-Hailing Apps: Grab and Gojek are just a few of the increasingly popular ride-hailing apps in Bali. These programs allow you to book a wide range of services, including car services, motorcycle taxis (commonly referred to as

"Gojek" or "ojek"), and even food delivery. They provide a simple and affordable way to go about the island, with the added advantages of transparent pricing and the capacity to follow your path.

3. Private Drivers: If you want a more individualised experience or want to visit a lot of things in one day, hiring a private driver is a great option. You may book a driver via your hotel, a travel agency, or online services. Hiring a private driver allows you to be flexible and explore off-the-beaten-path destinations at your own pace.

4. Renting a motorbike or scooter in Bali is a popular choice for those who are more brave. The traffic is simple to navigate, and it provides a chance for independent island exploration. Make sure you have a current international driver's licence, are wearing a helmet, and are familiar with local traffic rules and road conditions before renting a two-wheeler, however.

5. Bicycles: If you're searching for a more eco-friendly and active mode of transportation, renting a bicycle is a fantastic option. Bicycle rentals are available across Bali in locations like Ubud and Canggu. By riding a bicycle across the countryside, you can immerse yourself in the island's natural beauty, take in the stunning landscapes, and discover hidden gems.

6. Public Transportation: Although there aren't many options in Bali for public transportation, there are a handful. An affordable means of transportation in and around Denpasar is the bus service known as Trans Sarbagita. There are also bemos (minivans) and angkot (small public buses) in several regions of the island, mostly for usage by local commuters.

Walking: Due to its small size and charming districts, Bali is a good place to go for a stroll. Thanks to their well-maintained sidewalks, some well-known places, like Seminyak, Kuta, and Ubud, allow you to stroll to neighbourhood shops, restaurants, and attractions. In addition to enjoying the landscape, walking makes it possible to find hidden gems that may not be accessible by other forms of transportation.

When examining your options for getting about Bali, keep in mind your degree of comfort, your spending limit, and your preparation. Since each mode of transportation has benefits and downsides, choose the one that best satisfies your travel requirements and preferences. Bali offers a variety of transportation options to suit a wide range of visitors, ensuring that your journey to the island is as enjoyable as your final destination. These options include taxis, ride-hailing services, private drivers, motorcycles, bicycles, public transit, and even just walking.

# Chapter 3. Top Tourist Destinations

## *Ubud*

For travellers seeking a unique and instructive experience, the charming town of Ubud, which is situated in Bali's lush interior, is a must-see. The cultural hub of the island, Ubud, offers a seductive combination of spectacular natural beauty, traditional arts, serene spirituality, and kind hospitality. Because of its rich history, flourishing artists community, and appealing surroundings, Ubud has rightfully earned its place as one of the top tourist attractions in Bali.

Visitors are drawn to Ubud because of its picturesque surroundings, which include verdant rice terraces, roaring rivers, and dense forests. The town is the ideal retreat from Bali's crowded tourist attractions due to its tranquil atmosphere and stunning surroundings. A sight to see are the Tegalalang Rice Terraces, and visitors may also wander through the lush Monkey Forest, which is home to a merry troop of long-tailed macaques. In addition, there are stunning waterfalls in Ubud, like Tegenungan and Goa Rang Reng, where visitors may unwind and recharge while taking in the soothing sounds of running water.

In addition to its stunning natural surroundings, Ubud is also known for its thriving arts and crafts scene. There are several galleries, studios, and museums across the city that display both traditional and contemporary Balinese artwork. The work of talented local artisans who create gorgeous paintings, intricate wood carvings, and exquisite silver jewellery may be seen by visitors. The Ubud Art Market offers visitors the opportunity to look at and purchase one-of-a-kind handicrafts, textiles, and keepsakes that highlight the region's artistic talent.

For those searching for peace of mind, Ubud provides a serene retreat. In the town, there are several temples and retreat centres where visitors may take yoga and meditation sessions, learn about Balinese spirituality, or just relax and take in the calm and quiet. A few of the many sacred locations that beckon to travellers seeking seclusion and meditation are the well-known Goa Gajah (Elephant Cave) and the majestic Pura Taman Saraswati with its seductive lotus pond.

A vast array of restaurants dishing up delectable fusions of traditional Balinese flavours and foreign cuisines make up the enticing culinary scene in Ubud. Savoury regional dishes like babi guling (suckling pig), nasi campur (mixed rice), and refreshing tropical fruits are available for adventurous diners to try. In addition, Ubud is home to a number of culinary schools where visitors may learn how to prepare authentic Balinese dishes using fresh products from nearby markets and rice fields.

Due to the town's year-round cultural events and festivals, visitors get the chance to fully experience Balinese traditions and celebrations. The Ubud Authors and Readers Festival, Bali Spirit Festival, and Ubud Food Festival all attract artists, writers, musicians, and food enthusiasts from all over the world, creating a vibrant atmosphere and a swarm of creative activity.

The housing choices in Ubud include opulent resorts, welcoming guesthouses, and traditional Balinese residences, to name a few. The kind and welcoming inhabitants make guests feel at home and provide a genuine and thorough cultural experience.

In conclusion, Ubud on the island of Bali is a captivating site where tourists may discover the essence of Balinese culture, take in breathtaking natural beauty, and find inspiration and calm. Whether a visitor is seeking inspiration for their art, spiritual enlightenment, or just a relaxing holiday, Ubud offers an exceptional experience that will have a lasting impression on them.

## Kuta and Seminyak

Among the several regions of Bali, Kuta and
Seminyak stand out as two of the island's most
popular and sought-after tourist destinations.
Due to their unique blend of pristine natural
beauty, vibrant markets, exhilarating nightlife,
and sumptuous resorts, these areas have become
must-visit destinations for tourists from all over
the world.

Kuta, on Bali's southwest coast, is home to a
famed golden sand beach that is ideal for
swimming, surfing, and sunbathing. Excellent
waves and wide stretches of sand at the beach
attract surfers of all skill levels. With its
abundance of stores, street sellers, and shopping
centres offering everything from modern
clothing and accessories to traditional
handicrafts, Kuta is also a magnet for shoppers.
At night, Kuta comes alive with a thriving

nightlife scene, offering a wide range of entertainment options at many bars, clubs, and eateries.

Just north of Kuta, the wealthier and more affluent Seminyak is well-liked by those seeking a luxurious beach holiday. Seminyak's immaculate beach is well known for its stunning sunsets and azure waters. The area is noted for having upscale resorts, boutique hotels, and villas that provide first-rate amenities and customised services. Seminyak is also a foodies' paradise with its plethora of trendy restaurants and beach clubs serving both local and international cuisine. From upscale cafés to fine dining establishments, Seminyak's famed "Eat Street" is dotted with restaurants.

Both Kuta and Seminyak provide a wide range of activities and attractions in addition to their beautiful beaches. Due to the region's wealth of spas and health facilities, guests may enjoy spa treatments and wellness retreats. The Bali Bombing Memorial in Kuta serves as a sombre remembrance of the sad tragedy that occurred in 2002 and respects the lives lost in the terrorist attack. On the other hand, Seminyak is also known for its shops and art galleries that showcase the works of local designers and artists.

For those seeking adventure, Kuta and Seminyak serve as great jumping-off places for exploring the rest of Bali. Day excursions may be taken from here to other popular destinations like Uluwatu Temple, which is perched on a cliff overlooking the Indian Ocean, or Ubud, which is well-known for its lush rice terraces and cultural activities. For those interested in water activities like scuba diving, snorkelling, and jet skiing, several tour operators provide thrilling experiences.

In conclusion, Kuta and Seminyak are without a doubt two of Bali's most well-liked tourist spots. With their stunning beaches, vibrant nightlife, numerous shopping options, and luxurious hotels, these places provide a well-rounded experience that appeals to a range of interests. For all tourists, whether they are seeking relaxation, adventure, or cultural exploration, Kuta and Seminyak provide a taste of Bali's special charm and ensure an unforgettable holiday experience.

## *Nusa Dua*

Nusa Dua, located on Bali's southern coast, is without a doubt one of the most visited places by tourists visiting this tropical paradise. For those seeking the right mix of relaxation and activity, Nusa Dua, which is famed for its luxury resorts, spotless beaches, and first-rate amenities, offers an amazing retreat. It makes sense why tourists from all over the globe pick Nusa Dua due to its breathtaking beauty and variety of activities.

One of Nusa Dua's main draws is its stunning coastline, which has miles of fine, white sand and turquoise, crystal-clear waters. The beaches in this region are immaculate and well-maintained, offering a tranquil setting for swimming, tanning, and beachside picnics. Geger Beach, in particular, is a must-visit destination because of its serene ambience and stunning sunset views.

Nusa Dua is renowned for both its outstanding natural surroundings and its top-notch resorts and hotels. The area is home to numerous opulent hotels, many of which have spectacular villas, private pools, and top-notch service. Since these resorts often have their own private beaches, guests may have a unique experience. Numerous of them also provide a broad range of services, including spas, fitness centres, and numerous eating options, ensuring a really opulent stay.

Water sports enthusiasts also gather in Nusa Dua. The region's tranquil oceans and steady winds make it perfect for activities like sailing, diving, and snorkelling. To allow visitors to see the amazing underwater environment that is rich with colourful marine life, several dive companies provide excursions to nearby coral reefs. Due to the ideal conditions of the water, Nusa Dua is the ideal site for surfing, with waves that are appropriate for both beginner and professional surfers.

For those searching for cultural events, Nusa Dua doesn't disappoint. The Bali Nusa Dua Theatre hosts the enthralling Devdan Show in the area. This theatrical presentation highlights Indonesia's rich cultural past by fusing traditional dances, acrobatics, and special effects. This fascinating show offers a look into the numerous traditions and practices of the country.

Nusa Dua is a golfer's paradise with an 18-hole championship course set against a stunning beachside backdrop. The legendary golfers who designed the course gave players of all ability levels a challenging yet rewarding experience. Due to its immaculately kept greens and breathtaking views, Nusa Dua Golf & Country

Club is regarded as one of the best golf courses in Asia.

Nusa Dua is recognized for its cleanliness and safety in addition to its attractions. Due to the area's maintenance and the resorts' regular employment of stringent security measures, visitors may feel comfortable and protected. Due to the presence of international luxury hotel chains, the area also enjoys a reputation for expertise and service.

In conclusion, Nusa Dua is a well-liked traveller destination for Bali visitors because it offers the perfect blend of breathtaking natural beauty, luxurious accommodations, and exciting activities. If you're searching for world-class golfing, thrilling water sports, or just unwinding on stunning beaches, Nusa Dua has it all. It's hardly surprising that Nusa Dua is still a favourite option for travellers looking for an exceptional Bali holiday given its scenic surroundings and first-rate service.

# Jimbaran

Jimbaran is a captivating place that stands out as a top attraction for visitors to Bali. This little fishing village on the southwest coast of the island offers the perfect blend of breathtaking natural beauty, rich cultural heritage, and delectable cuisine. Because of Jimbaran's perfect beaches, gorgeous sunsets, and mouthwatering seafood, every visitor is assured an unforgettable experience.

One of Jimbaran's main attractions are the stunning beaches. The beachfront is surrounded by golden beaches and waves that are crystal clear, which creates a relaxing and excellent atmosphere for recreation. Visitors may enjoy sunbathing, leisurely strolls along the beach, and water activities like surfing and snorkelling. If you're seeking solitude or quality time with loved ones, Jimbaran's beaches provide a serene retreat from the hectic city life.

Along with its natural beauty, Jimbaran has a vibrant cultural history. The hamlet is home to a number of temples, including the well-known Pura Ulun Siwi, which has traditional Balinese architecture and serves as a place of worship for the locals. Visitors may get fully immersed in the spiritual atmosphere, witness the dynamic ceremonies, and discover more about Balinese customs and traditions.

However, Jimbaran's culinary delights are what truly set it apart. The town's seafood restaurants that line the shore are well-known. These eateries provide a wide selection of freshly caught seafood, including succulent grilled fish, juicy prawns, and succulent clams. The romantic meal experience is enhanced by the breathtaking sunset views. A seafood feast at one of Jimbaran's beachfront restaurants is a must for any foodie.

People searching for adventure may readily visit many nearby attractions from Jimbaran. You can reach the well-known Uluwatu Temple, which is perched on a cliff overlooking the Indian Ocean, after a little drive. Visitors may see the fascinating Kecak dance performance while admiring the temple's magnificent architecture. Also close are the vibrant nightlife and shopping districts of Kuta and Seminyak, which provide a wide range of entertainment options.

Jimbaran provides hotel options to suit every preference and budget. The perfect location for leisure and regeneration may be found among luxurious seaside resorts and charming boutique hotels, according to travellers. A total luxury holiday is guaranteed by the fact that many of these housing alternatives provide first-rate facilities including spas, infinity pools, and private villas.

In conclusion, Jimbaran is a lovely area that has earned its reputation as one of the top tourist destinations in Bali. With its pristine beaches, rich cultural heritage, delectable seafood, and simple access to other attractions, Jimbaran provides visitors of all ages with a diverse and rewarding experience. Whether someone is seeking adventure, relaxation, or culinary delights, this charming coastal village has a lot to offer.

## Denpasar

Denpasar, Bali's vibrant capital, serves as both the country's entrance point and a popular tourism destination for visitors to this Indonesian paradise. With its rich cultural past, beautiful views, bustling markets, and lively nightlife, Denpasar offers a unique and immersive experience for tourists wishing to discover the heart of Bali. Whether you're interested in history, art, gastronomy, or simply soaking up the local mood, Denpasar has a lot to offer everyone.

One of the must-see attractions is the Bali Museum, which is located in the heart of Denpasar. A substantial collection of artefacts and artefacts from Bali's colourful history are on display at this historical and cultural location. The museum provides a fascinating peek into the island's past by displaying everything from ancient stone sculptures to costumes and religious artefacts.

For those interested in traditional Balinese architecture, the Pura Jagatnatha temple is a magnificent example. The grand Sang Hyang Widhi Wasa temple is embellished with intricate stone carvings, strong gates, and beautifully landscaped grounds. Visitors to this sacred location are welcome to experience the spiritual ambiance while witnessing customary practices.

Another gem in Denpasar is the Badung Market, a hub of activity where locals and tourists gather to take advantage of the vibrant environment and shop for a variety of goods. The market offers customers a sensory extravaganza with everything from traditional batik and vivid textiles to fresh fruits, veggies, and spices. The market gives a chance to socialise, enjoy delicious street food, and discover one-of-a-kind items to take back home.

If you're seeking for a tranquil place to escape the hustle and bustle of the city, Denpasar boasts a lot of lovely parks and green spaces. The Bali Orchid Garden is a peaceful retreat with a huge collection of orchid species from all over the world. While strolling around the garden's walkways, visitors may learn about the delicate orchid growing process and take in the stunning flowers.

The vibrant nightlife of the city also plays a part in Denpasar's appeal as a tourist destination. The city comes alive after hours with a range of entertainment options, from trendy bars and nightclubs to locations to hear live music and see traditional dance performances. Whether you want to enjoy a quiet evening on the beach with a few beers or dance all night to the sounds of local DJs, Denpasar has it all.

A fantastic place to start exploring Bali's adjacent attractions is Denpasar. From here, guests may easily go to the beautiful beaches of Kuta, Seminyak, or Sanur for a day of surfing and sun. Accessible cultural landmarks in Ubud include the acclaimed Monkey Forest and its renowned art markets. Due to its advantageous location, Denpasar makes day trips to Tegalalang's breathtaking rice terraces as well as Uluwatu and Tanah Lot majestic temples simple.

Denpasar is a popular vacation spot for visitors to Bali due to its vibrant nightlife, bustling markets, rich cultural past, and advantageous location for seeing the rest of the island. Denpasar offers a range of attractions that will intrigue you and entice you to return, whether your interests are in history, art, food, or just wanting to immerse yourself in Balinese culture.

# Sanur

The little beach hamlet of Sanur, located on the southeast coast of the island, has long been one of Bali's most popular tourist attractions. With its stunning beaches, serene atmosphere, and rich cultural past, Sanur offers a different and amazing experience for those seeking a more relaxed and authentic Balinese vacation.

Sanur's breathtaking coastline is only one of the many things that set it apart as a well-liked location. The sandy beaches provide a serene and beautiful setting for water sports, swimming, and sunbathing. They are surrounded by palm trees that swing. In contrast to other larger beaches on Bali, Sanur's shoreline is still remarkably deserted, providing visitors a sense of tranquillity and privacy. Sanur Bay is ideal for diving and snorkelling because of its calm seas, and its vibrant coral reefs are home to a variety of marine life that is just waiting to be found.

In addition to its stunning natural surroundings, Sanur is known for its rich cultural heritage. Traditional Balinese temples may be found all across the city, providing visitors with a glimpse of the island's illustrious religious heritage and stunning architecture. Pura Segara, which is perched on a cliff overlooking the ocean, and Pura Blanjong, which possesses ancient inscriptions from the ninth century, are two of the most significant temples in the area. Visitors may get a complete understanding of the vibrant local culture by participating in regularly scheduled cultural activities and customs.

The relaxed atmosphere of Sanur is another aspect that makes it a popular tourist destination. Sanur offers a more relaxed and peaceful ambiance in contrast to the hectic nightlife and party scene of other parts of Bali. The town is full with quaint cafés, beachfront restaurants, and boutique shops, making it a great place for leisurely strolls and relaxed days. The Sanur Village Festival, an annual celebration of the community's arts, culture, and sports, strengthens the feeling of belonging and offers guests a chance to get to know local culture.

For those who are interested in exploring outside of the town itself, Sanur is an excellent place to begin further research. The nearby islands of Nusa Lembongan and Nusa Penida provide easy access, breath-taking natural landscapes, crystal-clear waters, and opportunities for water activities like cliff jumping, surfing, and snorkelling. Sanur is also readily reachable from other popular Bali tourist destinations like Ubud, Seminyak, and Kuta, allowing for day trips and excursions.

Sanur also provides a range of accommodations to suit the needs and preferences of every guest. The region offers a range of hotel choices, from luxurious beachfront resorts to cost-effective guesthouses. Numerous resorts provide breath-taking ocean views, first-rate facilities like spas, pools, and seaside restaurants so that visitors can relax and enjoy their stay.

In conclusion, Sanur is a popular Bali tourist destination because of its beautiful beaches, rich cultural past, laid-back atmosphere, and convenient location. Whether someone is seeking adventure, relaxation, or a stronger sense of community, Sanur has something to offer. With its unique blend of natural beauty and cultural appeal, Sanur continues to wow tourists from all over the world.

## *Candidasa*

For travellers seeking a tranquil and authentic Balinese experience, Candidasa on Bali's eastern coast has emerged as a hidden gem. For those looking to get away from the crowds and experience Bali's true essence, Candidasa offers a special and off-the-beaten-path setting thanks to the island's breathtaking natural beauty, extensive cultural history, and relaxed atmosphere.

One of Candidasa's most alluring attractions is its stunning coastline. Candidasa is the perfect place to unwind since it has a calmer and more serene atmosphere than Bali's more popular beaches. The clear waters and golden beaches, which are bordered by swaying palm trees, entice visitors to cool down or partake in aquatic activities like fishing, snorkelling, and diving. The underwater environment in Candidasa is a haven for divers due to its reputation for stunning coral reefs, vibrant tropical species, and even the possibility of seeing sea turtles.

In addition to its natural beauty, Candidasa is also known for its rich Balinese heritage and culture. All around the region, there are historic temples where visitors may see local customs and learn about Bali's spiritual side. One of the must-see temples in the region is the Pura Luhur Lempuyang, which is located on Mount Lempuyang's slopes. Photographers love to visit this temple complex because it offers stunning all-encompassing vistas of the region.

Additionally, Candidasa serves as the starting point for excursions into Bali's cultural centre. The traditional Balinese villages where you may see how people live their daily lives are not distant from the town. Tenganan, one of Bali's oldest towns, offers a glimpse into the island's rich cultural heritage via its particular weaving techniques and conventional building methods. Visitors may see traditional dance performances and look around local markets for lovely items and souvenirs.

Amazing natural wonders surround Candidasa, asking to be explored by those seeking adventure. A short drive will take you to the Tirta Gangga Water Palace, a stunning collection of ponds and fountains set within verdant grounds. The palace is renowned for its peaceful atmosphere and is the perfect place for a leisurely stroll or a refreshing swim.

Candidasa offers a range of housing options, from luxury resorts to warm guesthouses, in addition to its natural and cultural attractions. Many businesses have breath-taking views of the ocean or the hills in the distance and were built with the environment in mind. The town's restaurants and local warungs provide traditional Balinese meals as well as recently caught seafood from surrounding fishermen.

Candidasa appeals to visitors because it may provide a genuine and immersive experience of Bali away from the hustle and bustle of other tourist hotspots. Due to its tranquil beaches, rich cultural past, and opportunities for adventure, it has become a well-liked destination for travellers seeking a true and off-the-beaten-path place in Bali. Whether visitors are looking for relaxation, cultural exploration, or outdoor adventures, Candidasa offers a little piece of paradise that will leave a lasting impression.

## Lovina

Despite the island's many unique spots, Lovina stands out as a major tourist attraction. Lovina, which is situated along Bali's northwest coast, offers a unique and tranquil experience that is quite different from the island's crowded tourist hotspots.

The lovely seaside hamlet of Lovina is a prime example of Bali's calm beauty. Anyone searching for a more laid-back and peaceful retreat will find it to be a haven. The town's main draw is its stunning black sand beaches, which stretch for many kilometres and provide visitors the chance to unwind and refresh while taking in the spectacular views of the Bali Sea.

Among Lovina's most enticing qualities are the regular dolphin sightings. Visitors may go on boat tours in the early morning to observe these gorgeous creatures playing in the clear waters. Imagine how thrilling it would be to be in the company of playful dolphins as they gracefully dive and leap into the sea, creating an experience that would leave you speechless in the midst of nature's wonders.

Lovina, which is known for its abundance of dolphins, is also home to vibrant coral reefs that are a refuge for lovers of snorkelling and scuba diving. Lovina is an excellent area to go scuba diving because of its calm seas and plenty of marine life. Snorkelers may enjoy vibrant coral gardens, while scuba divers can dive deeper to discover exotic species and even visit the well-known USS Liberty wreckage at nearby Tulamben.

Lovina's allure extends beyond its natural beauty along the coast. The hamlet is well known for its mesmerising sunsets. As the sun sets, the sky transforms into an amazing work of art with vivid hues, casting an ethereal glow over the placid waters. Every visitor to Lovina is mesmerised by the tranquillity and tranquillity that the sunset gives, making it a very lovely experience.

Additionally, Lovina offers a glimpse into the true Balinese way of life. All across the town are traditional fishing settlements where people go about their daily lives. Tourists may thoroughly experience the local culture by strolling around the villages, speaking with the hospitable locals, and even attending traditional festivities and dances. The friendly greetings and honest grins of the Balinese people lend yet another layer of charm to Lovina's allure.

The hot springs at Lovina are renowned for being the perfect place to relax and revitalise. Nearby and well-known for their curative properties are the Banjar Hot Springs. Since the hot springs are surrounded by dense vegetation, they provide a peaceful setting for therapeutic water baths and soothing spa treatments.

Lovina offers a range of hotel options to suit various preferences and price ranges. Everyone may find a place to stay, whether they choose luxurious beachfront resorts or warm guesthouses. Additionally, several resorts offer yoga and meditation retreats, allowing visitors to better appreciate Lovina's serenity.

In conclusion, Lovina stands out as one of Bali's top tourist destinations due to its outstanding blend of pristine natural beauty, authentic culture, and tranquil atmosphere. Whether it's dolphin sightings, underwater exploration, stunning sunsets, or immersing oneself in the local way of life, Lovina offers a lovely holiday that truly captures Bali's allure. For those seeking a respite from the hustle and bustle of more popular tourist destinations, Lovina is the perfect place to unwind, commune with nature, and create lifetime memories.

# Chapter 4. Exploring Nature and Adventure

## *Mount Batur and Mount Agung*

Bali, Indonesia is home to Mount Batur and Mount Agung, two well-known volcanoes that offer tourists breathtaking natural beauty and one-of-a-kind experiences. Whether you are an adventurer, a nature lover, or a world visitor, these majestic mountains have plenty to offer. You may make the most of your visit to Mount Batur and Mount Agung by using the following advice.

Mount Batur, which is 1,717 metres above sea level, is one of Bali's most popular tourist destinations. It is renowned for offering spectacular morning climbs that entice hikers from all around. To allow visitors to see a breathtaking sunrise as they near the summit, the climb often starts early in the morning.

Adventurers like the route since it is challenging yet manageable for most fitness levels.

Ascending Mount Batur takes two to three hours while passing through luscious green forests and volcanic beauty. As you ascend, you'll be rewarded with breathtaking panoramic views of Lake Batur and the surrounding area. The caldera, a huge crater produced by prior eruptions, is spectacular to see. You could enjoy a well-deserved breakfast and the beautiful views after you reach the summit.

For those seeking a more immersed experience, Mount Batur also offers the opportunity to take a soak in its natural hot springs. After a tough climb, you may relax and rejuvenate your tired muscles in the warm, mineral-rich waters. This is the perfect activity for unwinding and savouring the peace of the mountain environment.

The Balinese people hold Mount Agung in great respect spiritually and it is Bali's highest peak at

3,031 metres. It is considered to be the dwelling of the gods and is a crucial part of their religious rites. Only experienced hikers should tackle the challenging ascent of Mount Agung. The challenging trip, which is sometimes finished overnight, is rewarded with breathtaking views of the island and its neighbouring islands, Java and Lombok.

If you want to learn more about Indonesian culture, go visit the Besakih Temple, often known as the "Mother Temple," which is located on the slopes of Mount Agung. This ancient Hindu temple complex is the largest and holiest on the island, including more than 20 separate temples within its grounds. The structure houses religious rites and offers a glimpse into Bali's rich spiritual heritage.

Even though Mount Batur and Mount Agung both provide unparalleled experiences, it is essential to prioritise security and environmental protection. Before beginning any walk, it is suggested to hire a local guide who is familiar with the highlands and skilled at navigating the terrain. They could confirm that you are using the proper equipment and safety precautions.

In conclusion, Mount Batur and Mount Agung should not be missed by visitors to Bali. From taking in breathtaking sunrises to experiencing the island's rich cultural and spiritual heritage, these majestic mountains have a lot to offer. Whether you choose to walk to the summit or just admire Mount Batur and Mount Agung from a distance, their majesty and natural beauty will leave you with lasting memories of your time in Bali.

## *Bali Rice Terraces*

For travellers seeking a harmonious mix of natural beauty and cultural heritage that will make an impression on their journey around the enchanting island of Bali, the Bali Rice Terraces provide a captivating experience. While highlighting the island's exceptional agricultural traditions and magnificent settings, these terraces, known as "sawah" in the local dialect, provide a peaceful respite from the bustling tourist attractions.

The stunning Bali Rice Terraces, which can be seen all across the island, are proof of the ingenuity and skill of Balinese farmers. Precision engineering and meticulous gardening were used to chisel out these terraces from the mountains, transforming the steep slopes into cascading tiers of lush green fields. The terraces' breathtaking look is proof that nature and humans have been able to cohabit harmoniously for aeons in a delicate dance.

A popular location to visit rice terraces is Tegalalang, which is near to Ubud. As you enter Tegalalang, you'll be greeted with a breathtaking landscape of emerald green rice fields, palm trees, and traditional Balinese dwellings. Enjoy a leisurely stroll down the terraces as you see the labour-intensive farming methods that have sustained generations of Balinese farmers and take in the calm and tranquillity of the setting.

Another well-known place for rice terraces is Jatiluwih, which is situated in the middle of Bali's central highlands. Jatiluwih offers a real and unadulterated experience as a UNESCO World Heritage site that has mostly resisted commercialisation. One of the best examples of the sustainable agricultural practices ingrained in Balinese culture is the subak irrigation system employed on these terraces, which is renowned for dispersing water across the fields in an equal manner.

To really understand the mood of the Bali Rice Terraces, think about joining a guided trip around the surrounding area. You may stroll around the fields while taking in the calming sounds of nature and sometimes seeing a local farmer tending to his or her crops by following the twisting, narrow trails. One may learn vital information about the locals' way of life and the deeply embedded traditions that have maintained

Bali's agricultural heritage by engaging with them.

There are plenty of amazing picture opportunities at the Bali Rice Terraces. Photograph the terraced landscapes against Bali's beautiful mountains, catch the interplay of light and shadow on the terraces at sunrise or sunset, and take in the vibrant hues of the fields throughout the planting and harvesting seasons. Each photograph will convey the beauty and serenity of this specific agricultural scene.

Take advantage of the opportunity to explore the rice terraces and consume some of Bali's traditional cuisine. The best local ingredients are used to prepare delightful meals in a variety of neighbourhood restaurants in the adjacent villages, including fragrant rice harvested in the same fields. Enjoy the delights of Nasi Campur, a rice-based dinner with a choice of mouthwatering side dishes, or revel in the joys of bubur injin, a black rice porridge with a rich, nutty flavour.

As you bid the Bali Rice Terraces farewell, keep in mind the beautiful, captivating experience you had exploring Bali's natural beauty. The serenity and ageless appeal of these terraces serve as a constant reminder of the island's close links to its nature and culture. Therefore, whether you're a nature lover, a cultural tourist, or simply looking for quiet, the Bali Rice Terraces urge you to embark on an unforgettable journey through a landscape that is as beautiful as it is rich in history.

## Tegallalang Rice Terraces

Bali, Indonesia's Tegallalang Rice Terraces are a breathtaking illustration of the island's rich cultural heritage and beautiful natural settings. These terraces, which are strewn throughout the lush slopes of the Tegallalang hamlet, have made a name for themselves as a well-liked stopping point for travellers curious to experience Bali's traditional agricultural practices and magnificent environment. Given the stunning scenery and tranquil atmosphere of the Tegallalang Rice Terraces, no visitor to the island should miss this incredible experience.

The Tegallalang Rice Terraces' more than a thousand-year-old subak irrigation system is renowned for its intricacy and creativity. This outdated technology allows the farmers to control the water distribution effectively throughout the terraces, resulting in a harmonious coexistence of human productivity and the surrounding environment. As you go through the terraces, you will be able to observe the breathtaking sight of tiers of rice fields, each level skillfully carved into the contours of the earth. The bright shades of green are indeed a sight to see, providing several opportunities for shooting lovely images and appreciating nature's beauty.

To fully appreciate the Tegallalang Rice Terraces, it is advisable to take a walk around them. Spend some time exploring the cramped areas that link the terraces and provide a variety of vantage points. As you pass by, local farmers will be working in the fields; their conical traditional hats and friendly smiles add to the trip's allure. You could get insight into the inhabitants' way of life and the challenges they face in maintaining this long-standing agricultural tradition by speaking with them.

Those seeking a more authentic experience might choose to work in farming with locals. Many farmers invite visitors to help with the planting or harvesting of rice, giving them an up-close look at the traditions and daily activities of traditional Balinese agriculture. This engaging activity increases your sense of connection to the environment and its inhabitants while giving you a greater understanding of the labour-intensive upkeep required to maintain these terraces in place.

The Tegallalang Rice Terraces are not just a marvel of agriculture but also a vibrant hub for the arts. Along the pathways, there are many stalls and shops selling exquisite handcrafted items including intricate wood carvings, batik textiles, and traditional paintings. By purchasing their wares, you can support the local economy and bring a piece of Bali's distinctive cultural heritage back home.

While visiting the Tegallalang Rice Terraces, it is essential to respect the environment and the local culture. Given that the terraces are a UNESCO World Heritage site, it is imperative to leave no trace and refrain from damaging or destroying them. Respect for the Balinese way of life is also shown by dressing modestly and adhering to local traditions and customs.

Finally, Tegallalang Rice Terraces should be a top priority for visitors to Bali. From the amazing natural beauty of the terraces to the cultural insights gained by interacting with the locals, this unique site offers a one-of-a-kind and unforgettable experience. Spend some time alone on the terraces, capture the stunning view on camera, and return with lifetime memories. A wonderful gem of Bali, the Tegallalang Rice Terraces show the island's harmonious cohabitation of people and nature.

## Waterfalls in Bali

The most enticing natural attractions on Bali are its waterfalls. With its flowing rivers, lush surroundings, and serene environment, Bali's waterfalls offer travellers looking for adventure and calm a lovely experience.

In Bali, there are several waterfalls, each with a unique aesthetic appeal. One of the most well-known waterfalls on the island is the Gitgit Waterfall, which is located in the northern Bali town of Gitgit. This breathtaking waterfall creates a magnificent sight as it rushes down from a height of 35 metres while being framed by dense tropical foliage. Due to the area's constant chilly, revitalising mist, it is the perfect location for rest and meditation.

Another well-known waterfall is Sekumpul Waterfall, which is situated in the Buleleng region. Some people consider Sekumpul to be Bali's most beautiful waterfall since it consists of seven different waterfalls that all flow into a tranquil lake. To uncover this hidden gem, tourists go on a journey through breathtaking rice terraces and verdant valleys, taking in Bali's lovely environment.

The Tegenungan Waterfall in the Gianyar area is another popular tourist site. This waterfall offers a serene and beautiful view due to the dense flora that surrounds it. Visitors may choose to have a swim in the clear waters, relax on the rocks, or just take in the gorgeous beauty all around them.

Those seeking a riskier experience might choose Aling-Aling Waterfall. It is possible for visitors to this waterfall, which is close to the town of Sambangan, to explore a multitude of cascades and natural pools. If you're searching for a thrill, you may slide down natural rock slides or plunge into the invigorating pools from different heights. The lush foliage and vibrant plants in Aling-Aling further increase its allure, making it a must-visit place for adventurers.

In addition to being beautiful, the waterfalls in Bali are significant to the Balinese culture. Many people admire these waterfalls and believe they possess magical powers. Balinese people often go to these waterfalls as part of purification and washing rituals. The chance to see these rituals and discover the deeply held spiritual beliefs of the Balinese people provides visitors' waterfall encounters a cultural edge.

Hiring a local guide will ensure your safety, help you make the most of your waterfall exploration in Bali, and show you lesser-known waterfalls that are off the beaten path. Don't forget to pack the essentials for your waterfall activities, like a swimsuit, insect spray, and comfortable shoes.

In conclusion, seeing Bali's waterfalls may be a peaceful and enticing experience. These natural wonders, which range from the majestic Gitgit and Sekumpul waterfalls to the exciting allure of Aling-Aling, provide a refreshing escape from the bustling tourist areas. No matter whether you're seeking tranquillity, adventure, or cultural immersion, Bali's waterfalls will leave you speechless in the presence of their breathtaking magnificence. So make sure you take the chance to explore these fascinating waterfalls while you're in Bali.

## *Bali Marine and National Parks*

Bali's national parks and marine ecosystems are a must-see for tourists looking for a distinctive and immersive experience.

The Bali Barat National Park is one of Bali's most well-known marine parks. The northwest coast of the island is home to this park, which covers a total area of around 190 square kilometres and is home to a great variety of both plants and fauna. The park offers a variety of habitats to discover, including dense forests, mangrove swamps, and clean beaches.

Visitors to Bali Barat National Park have access to a variety of recreational opportunities. Divers and snorkelers will be astonished by the many aquatic animals that reside in these waters in addition to the vivid coral reefs. Waters in the park are crystal clean and provide exceptional visibility, making it a paradise for those who like photographing underwater pictures. Dive under the surface of the sea to explore the park's marine life, which includes rare manta rays and other species.

The park's sublime splendour will mesmerise nature enthusiasts. It's possible to witness cheerful monkeys swinging from tree to tree and endangered bird species, like the Bali starling, on guided tours through the verdant jungle. The park also includes Menjangan Island, which is renowned for its clean beaches and variety of aquatic life. Visitors looking for adventure are welcome to visit the island, which offers exhilarating snorkelling and diving options.

The Nusa Penida aquatic Park is yet another gem in Bali's aquatic crown. This park is located on the islands of Nusa Penida, Nusa Lembongan, and Nusa Ceningan, which are all to the southeast of Bali. The park's breathtaking scenery, soaring cliffs, and emerald waterways provide for an enticing setting for a variety of activities.

When diving enthusiasts visit the Nusa Penida Marine Park, their dreams come true. The park is renowned for its encounters with enormous manta rays, as well as other wonderful aquatic creatures including colourful reef fish and turtles. The peculiar mola mola, also known as the marine sunfish, is an animal that may grow to astonishing proportions, and for many tourists, diving with it is a pleasure.

The park provides risky activities like cliff jumping and snorkelling with enormous ocean manta rays for thrill-seekers. For outdoor activities like hiking, the park's distinctive terrain offers a beautiful environment where clifftop views and uncharted beaches beckon discovery.

In addition to these maritime parks, Bali Taman National Park is situated in the eastern portion of the island. This park displays Bali's diverse wildlife and offers some endangered species protection. For hikers and nature lovers, the park's volcanic mountains, lush woods, and breathtaking waterfalls provide a spectacular setting.

When you visit Bali Taman National Park, you witness an amazing world. Throughout the park, you may see the magnificent white Bali myna with its vibrant blue highlights. The general public is in great peril. Long-tailed macaques, barking deer, and maybe the rare Javan lutung can all be seen by visitors. Weary travellers may discover rebirth and regeneration in the scenic surroundings on walking routes that weave through deep vegetation to spectacular waterfalls like the fascinating Gitgit Falls.

In order to save Bali's fragile ecosystems and marine and national parks, responsible tourism is encouraged. Interacting with local tour guides and park rangers will improve the experience and assist environmental conservation efforts.

## *Scuba Diving and Snorkelling Spots*

Bali's clear waters and diverse marine life make it a great place for scuba diving and snorkelling. Whether you are an expert diver or a novice snorkeler, Bali's underwater environment offers unforgettable experiences. Here are some of the top spots on this Indonesian island for scuba diving and snorkelling.

One of Bali's most well-known diving spots is Nusa Penida. Several diving locations, including Manta Point and Crystal Bay, exist on the island of Nusa Penida, which is located southeast of Bali. Thanks to its permanent population of these graceful creatures, Manta Point offers divers the chance to see magnificent manta rays up close. However, Crystal Bay is well known for both its exceptional visibility and the chance of seeing the rare Mola Mola, or sunfish.

Tulamben is another popular diving spot, particularly among enthusiasts of wreck diving. Here is the USAT Liberty, a World War II shipwreck that serves as an artificial reef and is now the setting for a healthy aquatic environment. As you explore the ruins, you'll come across colourful corals, schools of fish, and intermittent sightings of barracudas and reef sharks.

Menjangan Island in the West Bali National Park is a must-visit for divers seeking a unique diving experience. Beautiful coral reefs and a variety of aquatic life may be found on the island. The focal point of Menjangan Island is the Pura Ped underwater temple, which provides an excellent environment for underwater photography and exploring.

Tulamben and Menjangan Island are only a few of the numerous diving locations Bali has to offer. Amed, a magnificent location on Bali's northeast coast with vibrant coral gardens and a lively marine life. Off the shore of Amed, there is a Japanese Shipwreck that is often visited by divers.

Bali will not disappoint you if snorkelling is more your style. Padangbai's Blue Lagoon is a snorkeler's paradise with calm waters and an abundance of colourful tropical species. You could easily spend hours here getting up close to strange aquatic animals and enjoying the vibrant coral gardens.

Further east, the renowned snorkelling site of Nusa Lembongan beckons with its pristine waters and plethora of coral reefs. Jungut Batu and Mushroom Bay are well-liked starting points for snorkelling trips since you can swim with frolicking tropical fish there and maybe even get a glimpse of a few sea turtles.

You shouldn't miss the rich aquatic life in the area of Bali's Gili Islands. The Gili islands—Gili Trawangan, Gili Meno, and Gili Air—are each well known for their exceptional snorkelling opportunities. Swim through coral gardens, see clownfish in their natural habitat, and explore coral gardens as you become enthralled by the vivid marine life that exists in these waters.

Verify that experienced guides or instructors that prioritise environmental preservation will be joining you before you start your Bali scuba diving or snorkelling tour. Respect the marine ecosystem by avoiding contact with or damage to coral reefs or marine life.

Visitors may get a glimpse of the world below the water's surface, where vibrant coral gardens, schools of tropical fish, and exotic marine life abound, at Bali's diving sites and snorkelling spots. If you dive alongside stunning manta rays, explore submerged shipwrecks, or just enjoy the underwater environment, Bali's underwater treasures are sure to steal your breath away and leave you with lifetime memories.

## Surfing in Bali

For those seeking an unforgettable experience, Bali offers some of the best surfing opportunities in the world. The warm tropical waters, consistent waves, and breathtaking scenery attract surfers from all over the globe to this island paradise.

Due to the wide range of surf spots that are accessible and can accommodate surfers of all skill levels, Bali becomes the perfect holiday destination for both beginner and experienced surfers. Due to the island's diverse coastline, which provides a range of waves ranging from gentle beach breaks to fierce reef breaks, there is something for everyone. Some of the most well-known surfing spots are Kuta Beach, Uluwatu, Canggu, and Padang Padang.

Kuta Beach is located in the bustling town of Kuta and is famed for its long, sandy beach and beginner-friendly surf. To catch their first waves, beginners may rent surfboards or take lessons from local surf pros. Due to its vibrant atmosphere and vibrant nightlife, Kuta has a strong surfing culture that attracts surfers from all walks of life.

Uluwatu, located on the westernmost tip of the Bukit Peninsula, is a prominent surfing spot renowned for its challenging waves and magnificent cliff-top views. The famed Uluwatu wave breaks on a coral reef, providing skilled surfers with a spectacular ride. With beautiful cliffs and the well-known Uluwatu Temple around it, this surf spot offers a unique and breathtaking experience.

Surfers have become used to the trendy beach town of Canggu in southern Bali. Its black sand beaches and consistent waves make it the ideal place for surfers of all skill levels. After a fantastic session in the water, surfers may unwind at one of the seaside cafés and enjoy the laid-back atmosphere for which Canggu is known.

If you're searching for a tremendous surfing challenge, go to Padang Padang. Some of the best surfers in the world go to Padang Padang on the Bukit Peninsula to catch the renowned "Padang Padang Left" wave. Even the most seasoned surfers need to have the self-assurance and skills to handle the barreling waves at this reef break.

In addition to having world-class surf breaks, Bali also has a vibrant surf culture that improves the surfing conditions there. Tourists may easily take up surfing because of the island's availability of surf shops, board rentals, and surf courses. Festivals, competitions, and other events that emphasise the prowess and fervour of the regional and international surf scene are also part of the year-round surfing calendar.

Bali offers tourists a wide range of extra attractions in addition to the exhilarating surf experiences. With its historical temples, lush rice terraces, mouthwatering Balinese cuisine, and magnificent beach resorts, Bali is a destination that appeals to all interests and preferences.

Bali is a popular surfing location, but it's important to respect the area's ecosystem and culture. Surfers should be aware of local rules, which include avoiding crowded breaks, adhering to local surf traditions, and being mindful of their impact on the sensitive marine ecology.

Beyond the sport itself, surfing in Bali is enjoyable. It provides an opportunity to connect with nature, live the carefree Balinese lifestyle, and make lifelong memories. Whether you are a seasoned surfer or a beginner hoping to catch your first wave, Bali ensures a great experience that will make you want to visit its beaches again. So grab your board, hit the waves, and discover Bali's captivating surf scene.

# Chapter 5. Cultural and Historical Sites

## *Uluwatu Temple*

Uluwatu Temple is a fascinating historical and cultural landmark in Bali that charms visitors. It is perched on a breathtaking cliff edge with a panoramic view of the vast Indian Ocean. The Balinese people place a high importance on this old temple because it offers a glimpse into their rich cultural heritage and religious beliefs. It is situated on the southwest tip of the island. Uluwatu Temple, with its breathtaking views, stunning architecture, and exciting religious activities, is a must-visit venue for anybody interested in learning more about Bali's cultural and historical riches.

Uluwatu Temple, one of the island's oldest temples, with a history dating back to the 11th century. The temple is attributed to the Javanese philosopher Empu Kuturan, who had a significant impact on the development of Bali's religious practices. The temple has undergone several renovations and repairs throughout the years, yet its core spiritual values remain unchanged. One of the nine directional temples supposed to protect the island from evil spirits is Uluwatu Temple, which is dedicated to Sang Hyang Widhi Wasa, the supreme god of Balinese Hinduism.

The beautiful architecture of Uluwatu Temple is amazing. The ornate sculptures and carvings that adorn the black coral-stone structure depict both mythical animals and events from ancient Hindu epics. As they wander the temple grounds, visitors are greeted with intricately carved "candi bentar" gates and massive "meru" shrines. A photographer's and art enthusiast's paradise, Uluwatu Temple seamlessly blends natural beauty with human achievement.

Uluwatu Temple offers visitors the chance to see Kecak dance performances, a kind of traditional Balinese dance, in addition to its stunning architecture. As the sun sets and the waves smash in the distance, performers in colourful costumes fascinate the audience with their rhythmic chants and challenging dances. The Ramayana episodes in the Kecak dance provide a glimpse into the cultural traditions and narrative techniques that have been passed down through the millennia.

In addition to its cultural and historical significance, Uluwatu Temple's location adds to its allure. From its elevation on a steep rock that rises around 70 metres above the ocean, the temple provides expansive views of the adjacent coastline. During spectacular sunsets, the sky turns into a work of art with vibrant colours, casting a golden glow over the temple and the raging waves below. Surfers visit the temple because of the area's reputation for delivering waves of the greatest class.

It is imperative to adhere to the temple etiquette and dress modestly while visiting Uluwatu Temple as a sign of respect for the religious traditions and beliefs of the Balinese people. Sarongs are available for hire at the entrance for anyone who needs to conceal their legs. Additionally, visitors should stay away from the local monkeys of the temple complex due to their propensity for mischief.

Uluwatu Temple, a cultural and historical monument in Bali, enables tourists to delve into the island's rich spirituality and history. With its ancient origins, stunning architecture, captivating dance performances, and breathtaking views, this iconic temple offers an immersive experience that combines history, art, and natural beauty. Visitors to Uluwatu Temple leave with precious memories and a deep admiration for the island's many customs. An interesting journey into the centre of Balinese culture.

## Tanah Lot Temple

Tanah Lot Temple stands out as a historical and cultural treasure that no traveller should overlook among Bali's numerous appealing attractions. This ancient Hindu temple, perched on a rocky islet not far from the sea, offers tourists a unique and mind-blowing experience that immerses them in Bali's interesting history and spiritual traditions.

historic location Many myths and tales centre around the Tanah Lot Temple. It may be dated to the fourteenth century, when a Javanese priest named Danghyang Nirartha made a pilgrimage to Bali. Folklore has it that he landed at this beautiful spot and decided to build a temple for the sea gods. Since the temple seems to float on the ocean during high tide, Tanah Lot, a Balinese term that translates to "Land in the Sea" in

English, perfectly captures the stunning location of the temple.

Tanah Lot Temple's construction is a stunning illustration of Bali's cultural ingenuity. The temple's elaborate carvings and patterns showcase the island's distinctive architectural design. The temple was built from black lava stone. The main sanctuary, which is part of the temple complex's collection of shrines, is dedicated to the Balinese sea goddess Dewa Baruna. Discover the grounds of the temple and see the opulent decorations that decorate its buildings to witness the superb workmanship firsthand.

Tanah Lot Temple has cultural significance for the Balinese people in addition to historical significance. One of the seven sea temples, also known as sea chains, that extend down the southwest coast of Bali and are said to guard the island spiritually. Hindus in Bali revere Tanah Lot Temple as a holy place, and residents often go there to make sacrifices and practise their religion. Being there for these religious rites may be a very poignant experience that helps visitors get a greater appreciation for the island's spiritual practices.

Tanah Lot Temple is a well-liked site for photographers and outdoor enthusiasts because of its breathtaking sunset vistas. The landscape changes into something rather beautiful as the sun sets, illuminating the temple and the nearby body of water with a golden light. One can observe the unusual form of the temple against the vivid colours of the sky from vantage points along the cliffs or on the coast. They'll never forget how lovely it was to watch the sunset at Tanah Lot Temple.

The area around Tanah Lot Temple has been transformed into a bustling cultural park in order to improve the overall experience of tourists. The region's markets, art galleries, and restaurants, where diners may sample Balinese cuisine, are open to visitors. Theatre, music, and traditional dance performances are among the frequent cultural activities held in the park. The chance for tourists to fully immerse themselves in Bali's arts and culture and get a better understanding of the island's cultural traditions is fantastic.

Last but not least, Tanah Lot Temple is a magnificent historical and cultural location that visitors to Bali shouldn't miss. It is a fascinating place for history fans, lovers of beautiful architecture, and anybody interested in learning more about Balinese culture due to its historical roots, spectacular architecture, and spiritual importance. The beautiful surrounds around the temple provide an impressive visual spectacle as well, particularly at dusk. In Bali's heart and soul, Tanah Lot Temple offers a glimpse into a world where tradition, spirituality, and the natural world coexist.

## *Besakih Temple*

Bali's Besakih Temple, a stunning historical and cultural landmark located on the sides of Mount Agung, captivates visitors from all over the world. The largest and holiest temple complex on the island, Besakih, also known as the "Mother Temple of Bali," has a lengthy history.

Hinduism in Bali reveres the Besakih Temple, which was built in the ninth century. With the current structure being constructed in the fourteenth century, it is believed to have been a place of worship since the Stone Age. Over 20 separate temples, each dedicated to a different deity, make up the vast temple complex. The most venerated site in Besakih is said to be the centre temple, Pura Penataran Agung.

The architecture of the Besakih Temple is stunning. The towering pagodas, exquisitely carved stone gates, and brilliantly adorned shrines are stunning examples of the Balinese people's incredible craftsmanship and great attention to detail. With the use of black volcanic rock, red bricks, and thatched roofs, the temples are constructed in the traditional Balinese style, fitting in seamlessly with the landscape.

Besakih Temple offers a unique glimpse into Balinese culture and religious practices, so going there is about more than just admiring the stunning building. Hindus in Bali hold the Besakih Temple in high respect and hold many of their religious ceremonies and rituals there. Visitors may see devotees performing in rites, making offerings, and participating in prayers and ceremonies while clothed in traditional Bali attire.

By touring the temple complex, visitors may learn about the traditional Balinese religious practices and traditions. The intricate stone carvings depict scenes from Hindu epics including the Ramayana and the Mahabharata while telling stories of gods, demons, and heroes. Because of the comprehensive explanations and interpretations provided by the knowledgeable local guides, Besakih trips are very enlightening.

Besakih Temple not only has spiritual significance, but also offers breathtaking 360-degree views of the surroundings. The temple complex provides a vantage point from which to see the splendour of Bali's natural beauty since it is positioned on Mount Agung's slopes. Peace and tranquillity are fostered by the stunning backdrop of beautiful rice terraces, cascading waterfalls, and distant volcanoes.

It is advised that visitors to Besakih Temple dress modestly and with respect since it is a holy site. Sarongs and sashes are available for hire at the entrance for those who need them. It's also advisable to hire a local guide in order to fully understand the temple complex's historical and cultural significance.

Finally, Besakih Temple is a well-known illustration of Bali's vibrant culture and extensive history. Due to its historical origins, stunning architecture, and spiritual environment, it offers a valuable experience for tourists seeking a deeper understanding of Balinese culture. Besakih Temple is more than just a destination to take in the sights; it offers a journey into Bali's heart and soul.

## *Goa Gajah*

Goa Gajah, also known as the Elephant Cave, is one of Bali, Indonesia's most amazing historical and cultural sites. Visitors may get a fascinating glimpse into the lengthy history of the island in this ancient cave complex, which is near to Ubud. Goa Gajah is a must-see place for anyone who are interested in history and culture because of its beautiful carvings, serene surroundings, and spiritual significance.

The name "Goa Gajah" means "Elephant Cave" in English, despite the fact that there aren't any actual elephants within the cave. The cave received its name from the stone sculpture of an elephant that formerly stood at the entrance. It is believed that this monument was erected in the 1950s, many years after the cave was really built, in an attempt to attract tourists and give the region its well-known name.

According to legend, Goa Gajah has been a centre for spiritual pursuits since the eleventh century. The cave, which was carved out of a solid rock wall, is the main attraction of the location. The mouth of the enormous, menacing visage that forms the cave's entrance serves as the entrance. Visitors will discover a little chamber filled with stone idols, lingams, and a sacred bathing pool after they enter, concealed in the interior's faint lighting.

The stunning sculptures that can be seen everywhere around Goa Gajah are proof of the Balinese people's artistic prowess. Bas-reliefs depicting various mythical creatures, such as demons, gods, and beautiful celestial nymphs known as apsaras, are painted on the cave walls. These sculptures are thought to represent the descent into the underworld and the forces of good and evil.

Visitors may visit a serene and beautiful region outside the cave at Goa Gajah. The area around the cave complex is covered with lush flora, tranquil streams, and old stone structures. A tranquil meditation space and many little temples are also present at the spot, providing visitors with an opportunity to relax and practise spiritual reflection.

For those interested in learning more about Balinese culture and spirituality, Goa Gajah is a widely renowned sacred place. Despite its deep-rooted Hindu heritage, the area has also been influenced by Buddhism, as seen by the presence of a huge stupa nearby. This blending of religious customs makes the location more appealing and identifies it as an example of Bali's cultural diversity.

By visiting Goa Gajah, one may thoroughly immerse oneself in the rich tapestry of Balinese history and culture. The location's historical significance, gorgeous carvings, and serene ambiance combine to make for a really unique experience. The relevance of the cave complex may be better understood by visitors by hiring a local guide who can provide fascinating stories and insights about it.

Last but not least, Goa Gajah, often referred to as the Elephant Cave, is an intriguing historical and cultural site that should be on every visitor's itinerary when visiting Bali. With its ancient rock carvings, spiritual atmosphere, and lush surroundings, the place offers a particular view into Bali's past and its rich cultural heritage. Goa Gajah is not simply an intriguing series of caves to explore; it's also a site where you may get closer to the island's spiritual centre and discover more about Balinese culture.

## Tirta Empul Temple

Tirta Empul Temple, a historical and cultural landmark in the heart of Bali, enchants travellers from all over the world. By visiting this revered temple, which has tremendous significance for the Balinese people, visitors may get a unique perspective into the island's rich history, potent spirituality, and profound cultural traditions. Because of its serene setting, stunning architecture, and holy bathing waters, Tirta Empul Temple is a must-visit destination for anyone seeking an immersive and authentic Balinese experience.

One of Bali's oldest and most revered temples, Tirta Empul Temple, has origins that go back to the tenth century. The Warmadewa dynasty built the temple, which was dedicated to Vishnu, the Hindu god of preservation. According to local legend, the holy spring in the temple was created by the deity Indra in order to rejuvenate his troops. It is said that the holy water at the spring has purifying and therapeutic properties, attracting both devotees and curious tourists.

The temple's architecture showcases the exceptional craftsmanship of ancient Bali. Visitors are transported to a bygone era by the beautiful stone carvings, magnificent gates, and gorgeous pagodas in the temple complex. The complex decorations and figurative patterns depict stories from Hindu mythology while illuminating the deeply held spiritual beliefs of the Balinese people.

One of Tirta Empul Temple's main draws is its "pura beji," or bathing springs. Each section of these pools has been divided into smaller sections with a specific ceremonial or usage in mind. The "melukat," or cleansing ritual, which involves submerging oneself in the spring's crystal-clear water while going through a series of purifying rites, is urged for visitors to participate in. Visitors may connect with

Balinese spirituality and learn more about the island's culture via this interactive experience.

Tirta Empul Temple is especially beloved to the Balinese as a reflection of their independence and tenacity, in addition to its historical and spiritual significance. The temple has stood the test of time and outlasted several political changes as well as earthquakes and volcanic eruptions. It serves as a symbol of Bali's residents' enduring traditions and unwavering faith.

Tirta Empul Temple offers visitors the ability to engage with locals and see their devotion up close and personal, making it more than just a glimpse into the past. The temple complex is often bustling with activity as locals dress in traditional attire to participate in rites, make sacrifices, and pray. The vibrant atmosphere and the sight of devotees completely engaged in their spiritual pursuits provide visitors a powerful and captivating experience.

With its beautiful surroundings of lush green rice fields, Tirta Empul Temple is a haven of peace and tranquillity. On the temple grounds, visitors may take a leisurely stroll around the many shrines and pavilions or just find a quiet spot to meditate and soak in the spiritual ambiance.

To sum up, Tirta Empul Temple is a testament to Bali's rich historical and cultural past. Because of its ancient architecture, holy bathing waters, and significant spiritual significance, it is a must-visit place for anybody who wants to delve into the island's rich traditions. Everyone who enters the temple is left with a lasting impression as a result of the serene and immersing experience it offers, which transcends its historical and theological value. A journey through time and a glimpse into Bali's soul may be had by visiting Tirta Empul Temple.

## Bali Museum

The Bali Museum, one of Bali's top tourist destinations, is a significant historical and cultural site that fascinates guests with its eclectic collection and engaging displays. The museum, which was established in 1932 and includes a substantial collection of artefacts, works of antiquity, and traditional crafts, offers an enthralling glimpse into Bali's past.

The Bali Museum is located in the heart of Denpasar, Bali's capital city, in a large traditional building that showcases spectacular Balinese architecture. The many pavilions, courtyards, and gardens across the vast complex work together to create a cosy ambiance that transports visitors back in time. The museum's major goal is to preserve and present Bali's cultural heritage for both locals and tourists, giving them a comprehensive understanding of the island's history, art, and traditions.

As soon as they enter the Bali Museum, visitors are greeted with a range of exhibits that illustrate Bali's rich cultural past. The museum's several exhibit spaces each focus on a distinct aspect of Balinese culture. One of the most prominent locations, the Ethnographic Hall, has a wide variety of traditional Balinese antiquities, including intricate textiles, out-of-date equipment, and ceremonial items. These artefacts provide information on past rituals, customs, and island life in general.

Another significant section of the museum is the Archaeological Hall, which exhibits a range of archaeological discoveries from various time periods, including prehistoric times. While admiring the ancient pottery, bronze statues, and stone sculptures, visitors may learn about Bali's ancient civilizations. Traditional Balinese paintings and sculptures that highlight the island's unique creative legacy may be seen in a separate area of the museum. The art collection in the museum is really extremely interesting.

In addition to its permanent exhibits, the Bali Museum also offers temporary exhibitions, cultural performances, and educational events. These events encourage visitors to engage with the local community and increase their understanding of Balinese culture. Traditional dance shows, gamelan concerts, and lectures on traditional crafts are just a few of the educational options the museum provides.

In addition, the preservation of Bali's intangible cultural heritage depends on the Bali Museum. It actively collaborates with local organisations and traditional artists to preserve time-honoured artistic techniques including making batik, carving wood, and silversmithing. By offering these artisans a place to showcase their skills and educate future generations, the museum contributes to the preservation of Balinese traditions.

For those who want to learn more about Bali's unique cultural legacy, a visit to the Bali Museum is a must. Thanks to its wide exhibits, immersive environment, and exciting activities, visitors may enjoy a comprehensive experience that educates, amuses, and inspires them. Whether you are an art enthusiast, history buff, or simply curious about the island's rich history, the Bali Museum provides a remarkable journey through Bali's captivating past and vibrant present.

## *Pura Luhur Lempuyang*

Lempuyang Temple, also known as Pura Luhur Lempuyang, is an intriguing historical and cultural landmark that brings tourists from all over the world to the gorgeous island of Bali. The Balinese people place a high value on this famous temple, which is situated on Mount Lempuyang's slopes in East Bali. It also offers a view into the region's rich cultural heritage.

One of Bali's most revered and historic temples, Pura Luhur Lempuyang has a long and illustrious history. It was built in the eleventh century by the high priest Mpu Kuturan, who is credited with creating the island's holy setting. The temple complex had a number of alterations and expansions throughout time, improving its grandeur and aesthetic appeal.

One of Pura Luhur Lempuyang's most distinctive characteristics is its unusual split gate, also known as "Candi Bentar" in Balinese. The majestic entrance of the temple sets the tone for its great magnificence and offers a breathtaking view of the surrounding mountain range. Balinese Hindu mythology and beliefs are reflected in the gate's magnificent carvings and symbolic patterns.

Each of the several tier-style terraces, magnificent shrines, and pavilions that greet visitors as they make their way around the temple complex has a distinct spiritual significance. The temple's location atop Mount Lempuyang's slopes adds to its allure and creates a serene atmosphere perfect for reflection and meditation.

In addition to being a site of worship, Pura Luhur Lempuyang attracts pilgrims. It is the first of seven temples said to make up a sacred pathway up to Mount Lempuyang's summit. At the end of the route lies the final temple, Pura Luhur Lempuyang Luhur, which represents the accomplishment of every stage of the pilgrimage. Many worshipers undertake the arduous journey to pay homage to the gods and request favours.

Pura Luhur Lempuyang offers amazing panoramic views of the surroundings, including the beautiful Mount Agung, Bali's largest volcano, in addition to having historical and religious significance. Due to the temple's elevated location, visitors can take in stunning sunrises and sunsets, which enhances the allure and mysticism of the setting.

Those interested in learning more about Balinese culture have a unique opportunity to observe traditional religious rituals and ceremonies at Pura Luhur Lempuyang. Visitors may get a glimpse of the spiritual practices and beliefs that are important to Balinese culture by seeing people praying, offering gifts, and participating in elaborate rituals.

It's important to respect the temple's sacredness and adhere to the dress requirement while visiting Pura Luhur Lempuyang. To enter the temple grounds, you must dress modestly and don a sarong, a traditional wraparound garment. Hiring a knowledgeable guide who can explain the significance, history, and rituals of the temple may enhance the whole experience.

Finally, Pura Luhur Lempuyang in Bali is a historical and cultural gem that offers tourists a deep understanding of the island's spiritual and religious heritage. Due to its storied history, stunning architecture, and stunning natural settings, this sacred temple is a must-visit place for anybody wishing to develop a stronger connection with the cultural core of Bali.

# Chapter 6. Beaches and Islands

## *Balangan Beach*

The beautiful tropical sanctuary of Balangan Beach, which is situated on the southwest coast of the magnificent island of Bali, attracts visitors from all over the world. Due to its flawless white sand, clear waters, and breathtaking panoramic views, Balangan Beach is a must-visit destination for anybody seeking sun, sand, and peace.

Balangan Beach, which can be found in the middle of the Bukit Peninsula, offers a peaceful retreat from the crowded tourist areas of Bali. Due to its well-known, top-notch surf breaks, it is a haven for surfers. The consistent and powerful waves that pour in from the Indian Ocean attract surfers of all skill levels, creating a pleasant and lively surf scene. Whether you're a seasoned surfer or a beginner hoping to catch your first wave, Balangan Beach offers the perfect conditions for a great surfing experience.

Balangan Beach is well known for its stunning surroundings in addition to its amazing surf. Tall limestone cliffs that surround the beach add to its attraction by creating a dramatic backdrop. As you unwind on the soft sand or take a leisurely stroll down the shore, you will be amazed by the amazing natural beauty that is all around you. The beach is also littered with a variety of beachside bars and eateries where you can unwind with a delectable dish from the area or a cool beverage while soaking in the laid-back atmosphere.

If you're searching for a more subdued experience, there are a number of calm locations on Balangan Beach where you may unwind and re-establish touch with nature. Find a secluded spot on the shore, take in the sunshine, and listen to the waves gently crashing on the sand. The beach is a terrific place to relax and recharge since it is much less crowded than other of Bali's more popular tourist destinations.

If you're up for an adventure, have a look at the nearby cliffs and caverns. At low tide, it is possible to access some of Balangan Beach's hidden caves. Exploring these natural wonders will add more mystery and excitement to your beach holiday. You may also climb the short distance up the cliffs for a bird's eye view of the beach and its surroundings and a fantastic vantage point for magnificent sunset vistas.

When planning travel arrangements to Balangan Beach, it's important to bear in mind the absence of significant services like showers and restrooms. However, the simplicity and pure beauty of the beach contribute to its attractiveness by allowing you to lose yourself in nature and forget about the concerns of modern life.

Last but not least, Balangan Beach offers a slice of paradise that is sure to leave a lasting impression on each and every traveller. Whether you're seeking world-class surf breaks, breathtaking scenery, or a peaceful haven, Balangan Beach has it all. Due to its unrivalled natural beauty, kind hospitality, and laid-back attitude, this hidden gem in Bali is a location that should not be missed. Pack your bags and grab your surfboard and get ready for a fantastic trip to Balangan Beach.

## Padang Padang Beach

Padang Padang Beach on the lovely island of Bali is a must-visit destination for travellers seeking spotless white sands, clear waters, and a taste of a tropical paradise. Thanks to its breathtaking surroundings and world-class surf breaks, Padang Padang Beach offers the perfect mix of relaxation and adventure for beach lovers and surf enthusiasts alike.

On the Bukit Peninsula in Bali's southwest, Padang Padang Beach is conveniently adjacent to well-known tourist hotspots like Kuta and Seminyak. As you descend the lovely stairs that lead to the beach, you will be greeted with a picture-perfect view of towering limestone cliffs, swaying palm trees, and crystal-clear oceans. The beach is surrounded by a natural cove, which gives it a sense of seclusion and serenity.

One of the beach's main attractions is its reputation as a great surfing spot. Due to its well-known left-hand reef break, surfers from all over the globe swarm to the beach to ride the challenging waves. Padang Padang is an excellent location for both seasoned surfers and novices looking to learn the sport and give it a try because of its regularly high waves, especially during the dry season (May to October).

Even if you don't surf, Padang Padang Beach offers a lot of interesting attractions. You may relax on the soft beach while taking in the sunshine and the refreshing ocean breeze. The beach is a terrific location for photos that will appear well on Instagram because of the picturesque surroundings. In addition to the breathtaking cliffs and rock formations in the area, you can also explore tidal pools at low tide, which are brimming with fascinating aquatic life.

If you're feeling very bold, you may try scuba diving or snorkelling at the nearby reef. Padang Padang's stunning underwater environment, which is home to a variety of colourful coral reefs and tropical animals, offers an incredible aquatic experience. You may either sign up for a tour with a guide or rent snorkelling gear at the beach to get the most out of your underwater adventure.

There are several beach warungs (local eateries) that provide delicious Indonesian cuisine for when you need to refuel. There are many alternatives available to satisfy your palate, ranging from mouth watering Nasi Goreng (Indonesian fried rice) to freshly caught seafood that has been skilfully prepared. As you relax and enjoy your meal, take in the breathtaking ocean views.

Getting to Padang Padang Beach early in the morning or on a weekday may help you escape the crowd and get a decent beach position. It should be noted that Padang Padang Beach may become rather congested, especially during the peak tourism seasons. It's important to observe local customs and traditions when visiting Bali, like dressing modestly while away from the beach and being cautious with trash disposal to preserve the area's natural beauty.

In conclusion, Bali's enticing Padang Padang Beach is a slice of paradise. A paradise inside a paradise, if you will. Whether you're seeking for tranquil sunsets, exciting surf breaks, or underwater excursions, this beach has it all. Due to its amazing natural beauty and wide range of activities, Padang Padang Beach is a must-see for any traveller hoping to experience the best of Bali's coastal pleasures.

## Dreamland Beach

Dreamland Beach, nestled away on Bali's southern coast, is a true gem for tourists looking for beautiful white beaches, clean waters, and a sense of tranquillity in the midst of breathtaking natural beauty. This picturesque beach is a must-visit destination for anyone looking to get away from the hustle and bustle of everyday life and enjoy the calm of Bali's coastline.

The Pecatu area's Dreamland Beach is in a stunning location, with towering cliffs creating a dramatic backdrop for the glistening waters below. As soon as you set foot on the soft, powdery beaches, you'll be mesmerised by the breathtaking surroundings. The beach is about a kilometre long, providing visitors with plenty of space to unwind, soak in the sun, or take a leisurely stroll down the shore.

Due to its amazing wave breaks, Dreamland Beach is a favourite surfing location for surfers from all over the world. Surfers of all skill levels may enjoy the exhilarating experience of the breaking waves. If you've always wanted to attempt surfing, there are surf schools where you may take lessons from trained instructors and master the sport.

There are other options to Dreamland Beach for those seeking a more laid-back experience to unwind and regenerate. Pick a cosy spot on the beach, take in the warm tropical sun, and lose yourself in a good book. When the gentle sea breeze comes through, you'll feel more peace and tranquillity than you've ever known.

As you explore the beach, you may find several coastal cafés and restaurants that provide a relaxing eating experience. Take in the magnificent beach views while sampling the local cuisines. A broad variety of foods, including traditional Balinese dinners and dishes made with fresh fish, are available for you to pick from.

In addition to the beach, Dreamland features additional attractions that are well worth seeing. Only a short distance away is the well-known Uluwatu Temple, which is perched on a cliffside overlooking the Indian Ocean. As you see the magnificent Kecak dance performance at twilight against the temple's backdrop, you will be in awe.

If you like the game of golf, Dreamland is home to the 18-hole championship New Kuta Golf Course, which is famous for its challenging layout and breathtaking seaside views. As you hit the course among lush greens and magnificent vistas, create lifetime memories.

Dreamland Beach offers a range of accommodations to suit the requirements of every guest. From luxurious resorts to inviting guesthouses, you may choose lodging that meets your requirements and gives you easy access to the beach and its nearby attractions.

In conclusion, Dreamland Beach is a true paradise for travellers to Bali. With its beautiful beaches, inviting waves, and magnificent natural surroundings, this beach provides a tranquil retreat from the grind of everyday life. Whether you're searching for relaxation or adventure on the waves, Dreamland Beach offers an amazing experience that will make you want to return often.

## Gili Islands

The Gili Islands, a lovely archipelago off the northwest coast of Lombok Island, are becoming a must-see destination for visitors visiting Bali. These three little islands, Gili Trawangan, Gili Air, and Gili Meno, together known as these tropical paradises, provide a fantastic escape from Bali's bustling streets. With its beautiful white sand beaches, vivid turquoise oceans, and abundant marine life, the Gili Islands provide a unique and extraordinary experience for all types of travellers.

Gili Trawangan, the largest and most populated of the three islands, is often referred to as the "party island." It features a lively nightlife culture with bars along the beach, live music venues, and parties that go until the early hours of the morning. Thanks to the range of hotel options on the island, which range from costly guesthouses to lavish resorts, there is something for everyone. Along with nightlife, visitors may take part in a number of water sports including snorkelling, scuba diving, and surfing as well as take in stunning sunsets and views of Bali's Mount Agung.

If you're seeking for somewhere with a more tranquil and relaxed atmosphere, Gili Meno is the best choice. It is referred to as the "honeymoon island" because of its lovely beaches, beautiful waters, and serene surroundings that are ideal for romance and leisure. Visitors may take leisurely strolls down the beach, swim in the calm waters, or just unwind in one of the many hammocks scattered across the island. Additionally, Gili Meno has a lovely saltwater lake where visitors may enjoy the tranquillity of nature and witness a variety of bird species.

The vibrancy of Gili Trawangan and the calm of Gili Meno are effectively balanced on Gili Air. This island offers a more authentic and local experience because of its small population and slower pace of life. Visitors may find the island's undiscovered beaches, small-town cafés, and charming accommodations by riding a bicycle or wandering about. Hobbyists who like snorkelling and diving will enjoy the stunning coral reefs right off the coast of Gili Air, which are home to sea turtles and a variety of colourful fish.

One of the great draws of the Gili Islands is the absence of motorised transportation. Since cars and motorcycles are not allowed on the islands, visitors may enjoy a peaceful and pollution-free environment. Instead, bicycles and cidomos, or horse-drawn carriages, are the main modes of transportation on the islands. This enhances the islands' natural beauty and serenity.

When planning travel arrangements to the Gili Islands, it's important to bear in mind that much of Bali's infrastructure is lacking there. Electricity and internet access may not always be available. But it simply adds to the islands' rustic allure and makes it possible for tourists to disconnect from the outside world and truly appreciate their natural beauty.

The quickest ways to get from Bali to the Gili Islands are via fast boat or public ferry, with PadangBai and Serangan being the most popular starting points. The journey takes one to two hours, depending on the mode of conveyance.

In conclusion, the Gili Islands provide a slice of paradise to those seeking a tranquil retreat from Bali's bustling environment. If you're looking for a vibrant nightlife, quiet romance, or a combination of the two, the Gili Islands have it all. Anyone visiting Bali should be sure to stop in the Gili Islands because of its stunning beaches, an abundance of marine life, and unique island atmosphere.

## Nusa Penida

Nusa Penida, a hidden gem lying off Bali's southeast coast, may appeal to intrepid travellers hoping to get away from the bustling crowds of the mainland. It offers a memorable and stunning holiday experience. Nusa Penida has gained appeal as a holiday destination for those looking to truly experience Indonesia's natural grandeur because of its untamed beauty, spectacular landscape, and rich cultural past. Here, we examine the allure of Nusa Penida and the explanations for why every visitor to Bali needs to include it on their itinerary.

One of Nusa Penida's main attractions is its unspoiled beauty and natural surroundings. The island is home to breathtaking beaches, cliffs as high as the sky, and rolling hills covered with rich vegetation. Kelingking Beach, with its unmistakable T-Rex-shaped rock formation, the spectacular Angel's Billabong, and Broken Beach are just a few of the breathtaking sights that welcome visitors. Explore the island's rugged shores and hidden coves whether you're a nature lover or a photographer hunting for the perfect shot.

The island of Nusa Penida offers a wide range of adventure activities in addition to its natural beauty. One of the most popular activities is scuba diving or snorkelling in the vibrant coral reefs that surround the island. The area's underwater ecosystem is home to an abundance of marine life, including manta rays, turtles, and rare fish species. Experienced divers may explore the well-known Manta Point, where encounters with magnificent manta rays are almost guaranteed. Cliff jumping at Peguyangan

Waterfall or exploring the beautiful natural pools of Tembeling Forest are exhilarating adventures that thrill-seekers shouldn't miss.

In addition to being a haven for outdoor lovers, Nusa Penida has a vibrant cultural legacy that affects the daily lives of its residents. Visitors may thoroughly immerse themselves in the local culture by visiting traditional villages and taking part in Balinese ceremonies and rituals. On the island, there are several ancient temples, such as Pura Goa Giri Putri, which is housed in a limestone cave and offers a unique spiritual experience. The hospitable and polite people who are always eager to share their traditions and customs provide a very significant cultural experience.

On Nusa Penida, the trip itself is an adventure. The rugged terrain of the island demands tenacity and a desire to learn new things. Renting a scooter is a popular way to navigate the winding, twisty roads since it allows visitors to explore hidden treasures at their own pace.

Despite the infrastructure still being constructed, the island's rustic beauty and off-the-beaten-path attraction more than make up for any shortcomings.

There are a variety of hotel options on Nusa Penida, from opulent resorts to budget-friendly homestays, so there is something to suit any traveller's interests and price range. Numerous motels feature breathtaking ocean views, which provide a quiet and alluring backdrop for a genuinely relaxing getaway. The regional cuisine, an amazing blend of Indonesian flavours, is known for its fresh seafood. Try classic treats like sate lilit (grilled minced beef satay) and nasi goreng (fried rice) if you're a cuisine enthusiast looking to delight your palate.

Finally, Nusa Penida offers tourists to Bali a unique and unforgettable experience. Its natural beauty, adventurous activities, cultural heritage, and warm welcome make it a fantastic spot for anyone looking for an alternative to the well-known tourist sites. Whether you're a culture vulture, a nature enthusiast, or an extreme adrenaline junkie, Nusa Penida has something to captivate and inspire you. So be sure to include this untapped gem in your itinerary for Bali and get ready for an unforgettable experience that will have you itching to return.

## *Nusa Lembongan*

The lovely island of Nusa Lembongan, which is nestled in the tranquil seas of the Bali Sea, is only a short boat ride off Bali's southeast coast. For those looking for a calm refuge away from Bali's hectic throng, Nusa Lembongan, noted for its clean beaches, clear seas, and laid-back environment, is the ideal holiday destination.

Nusa Lembongan's paradisiacal environment will wow tourists with its unspoilt natural grandeur. Despite being just approximately eight square kilometres in size, the island is home to many breathtaking landscapes. Mushroom Bay,

Dream Beach, and Sandy Bay are just a few of the breathtaking white sand beaches where tourists may relax, soak up the sun, and cool down in the refreshing sea.

The amazing marine life is one of the island's key attractions. The island's spectacular coral reefs make it a haven for snorkelers and scuba divers. If you want to explore the vibrant underwater environment that is home to tropical fish, sea turtles, and even manta rays, don your snorkelling gear or sign up for a diving trip. Swim with these magnificent creatures at the renowned Manta Point, which is situated off the coast of Nusa Penida, Nusa Lembongan's neighbouring island.

Nusa Lembongan has everything an adventurer might desire. On a motorcycle or bicycle, explore the island's uninhabited interior to find secluded coves, thick mangrove forests, and breathtaking cliff top views. Devil's Tear is a must-visit location for magnificent vistas and fantastic picture opportunities since it is a natural rock structure that displays the unbridled strength of the smashing waves.

In Nusa Lembongan, tourists seeking a cultural experience may learn about the island's lengthy history and traditional way of life. Visit historic temples like Pura Puncak Sari and Pura Segara, meander through quaint villages, and observe traditional Balinese practices to experience the island's distinctive spiritual atmosphere. Don't pass up the opportunity to see a Balinese traditional dance performance where talented dancers vividly portray historical tales via their deft movements and striking costumes.

In Nusa Lembongan, there are several eating alternatives to suit every taste. There is something for everyone, from hip bars with energising drinks and live music to beach cafés serving fresh seafood and Indonesian specialties. For a special dining experience, try the regional specialty Nasi Campur, a meal of rice topped with a variety of small items such as meats, veggies, and sambal (hot sauce).

In Nusa Lembongan, lodging choices vary from opulent beachside villas to reasonably priced guesthouses. Find the ideal spot to unwind and recuperate on this island paradise by selecting between a tiny house surrounded by charming gardens or an extravagant resort with breathtaking ocean views.

Take a brief ferry from Sanur or Padang Bai on the island of Bali to Nusa Lembongan. Depending on the starting place, the trip might take up to an hour. Getting about the island is simple after you've arrived since most of the attractions are close to one another and simple to get there on foot, a bike, or a scooter.

In conclusion, Nusa Lembongan provides a tranquil and endearing haven for anybody seeking a piece of paradise when visiting Bali. This undiscovered jewel should not be overlooked because of its beautiful beaches, abundance of marine life, diversity of cultures, and laid-back environment. Nusa Lembongan has a lot to offer, whether you're a beach bum, an adventurer, or a cultural vulture.

# Chapter 7. Traditional Arts and Crafts

## *Batik and Weaving*

If you're a traveller who intends to visit the seductive island of Bali, be ready to immerse yourself in a world of vibrant cultural traditions and artistic activities. Among the many types of art that thrive on the island, batik and weaving stand out as exceptional representatives of the island's vibrant culture. These traditional crafts provide visitors a unique opportunity to learn about the island's history and participate in its creative legacy, in addition to demonstrating the amazing craftsmanship of the Balinese people.

The traditional Indonesian textile craft of batik uses a wax-resist colouring technique to produce intricate designs on cloth. Batik has a special place in the hearts of the people of Bali since it is a representation of the cultural identity of the locals. The artist starts the procedure by applying hot wax in specified patterns to the fabric using a canting, a little copper tool with a spout. The colour cannot penetrate the covered areas because the wax acts as a barrier. After that, the linen is submerged in natural dyes to create stunning patterns and vibrant colours. In the last step, the wax has to be taken off to reveal the beautiful motifs created by the artist's skilled hands.

Visitors may get a fascinating glimpse into the whole process at Bali's Batik workshops and studios. Ubud, which is regarded as the cultural hub of Bali, is where you can get batik. Meeting local artisans in person enables you to observe their meticulous work up close and possibly even try your hand at creating your own Batik masterpiece. Visitors may attend Batik classes where they can learn the techniques and create one-of-a-kind souvenirs to take home. Travellers may participate in a batik class to learn about the artistry of batik, support local artisans, and aid in the preservation of an antiquated art form.

Weaving is another well-known traditional technique practised by skilled artisans in Bali and has been done so for many years. The island's agricultural and spiritual traditions both have a strong influence on Bali's weaving culture. The craft involves joining threads in intricate patterns to create lovely fabrics with cultural significance. Cotton, silk, and natural fibres are just a few of the materials used throughout the weaving process.

To discover more about Bali's weaving business, tourists may stop by villages like Tenganan and Sidemen, which are renowned for their weaving cultures. Visitors visiting these communities may learn about the history of the themes and patterns as well as see the intricate weaving process in action. Balinese weavers often draw inspiration for their patterns from mythology, religious ceremonies, and nature, giving them a symbolic meaning.

Along with seeing the weaving process, tourists may support local weavers by purchasing their handcrafted textiles. Because of their vibrant colours, unusual patterns, and fine craftsmanship, these textiles make priceless keepsakes. Beyond simple decorations, these woven textiles may be turned into clothing, wall hangings, or accessories that serve as a souvenir of your trip to Bali.

Visitors may access Bali's traditional past via weaving and batik. These traditional arts demonstrate the ingenuity of the island and the Balinese people's dedication to maintaining its long-standing traditions. By experiencing Bali's batik and weaving industries, tourists may get knowledge about the cultural significance of each art form, see the intricate craftsmanship, and assist local artisans. By embracing these traditional arts, visitors may create lifetime memories and contribute to the preservation of Bali's creative legacy.

# Wood Carving

The practice of wood carving has a long history in Bali, Indonesia. Visitors to this enchanting island will find it intriguing to investigate the world of wood carving since it gives them the chance to see the skilled craftsmanship and rich heritage of the Balinese people. Everything from intricate sculptures to masterfully carved masks and furniture showcases Bali's creative creativity and its deep connection to spirituality via the art of wood carving.

Bali has a long history of being hailed as a hub for creativity, and its artisans are highly regarded for their mastery of the trade of wood carving. Bali has a rich tradition of woodcarving, including influences from the local mythology, Buddhism, and Hinduism. Balinese carvers often ascribe spiritual and metaphorical meaning to their creations because they see wood carving as a sacred art form.

One of the most famous locations for wood carving is the hamlet of Mas, which is close to Ubud, Bali's cultural centre. Mas is renowned for its skilled craftspeople who create exquisite sculptures out of various woods, including teak, mahogany, and ebony. While strolling through the alleyways of Mas, visitors will come across several studios and galleries that exhibit a range of intricate wood carvings, from traditional figures to contemporary designs.

Amazing levels of artistic skill and attention to detail may be seen in Bali's wood carvings. Over the course of several hours, artisans meticulously cut and shape the wood using different instruments including chisels, mallets, and rasps. The pieces' many decorative themes, delicate facial expressions, and exquisite patterns showcase the Balinese carvers' creative genius.

One of Bali's most recognizable examples of wood carving is the Barong mask. The Barong is a mythological character that represents good spirits and protects against evil in Balinese mythology. Religious ceremonies and traditional dance performances both make use of these masks. They are composed of wood and embellished with gold leaf and vibrant hues. Visitors may see the captivating Barong dance and marvel at the gorgeous masks, which are examples of the skill and creativity of the wood carvers.

In addition to carving masks, Bali's woodworkers also produce a wide range of sculptures, figures, and furniture. Intricately carved sculptures of gods and mythical creatures like Garuda, Hanuman, and Ganesha are available in a range of sizes and make wonderful keepsakes. Additionally, ornately carved furniture, doors, and panels highlight Balinese craftsmanship and give any home an air of exotic beauty.

For those who are interested in learning more about wood carving, there are several workshops in Bali that provide practical sessions where guests may see the art form firsthand.

Knowledgeable instructors lead the participants through the procedure while instructing them on wood selection, finishing techniques, and carving techniques. Visitors may create their own unique piece of Balinese art by participating in a wood carving workshop, which also increases their awareness of the art form.

Wood carving is intricately related to Balinese culture and provides a window into the island's lengthy artistic tradition. Don't miss the opportunity to learn more about the world of wood carving while visiting Bali, whether it is by attending exhibits and seminars, seeing traditional performances, or even taking a wood carving class. They'll do this to get a deeper understanding of Bali's vibrant artistic traditions and to take priceless works of art back home.

## Silver and Gold Jewelry

Bali is especially well-known for its exquisite silver and gold jewellery, which has turned into a must-buy for many travellers that visit the island. If you're looking for a particular souvenir or are a seasoned jewellery collector, Bali provides a vast selection of goods to suit your preferences.

Silver jewellery is emphasised especially in Bali's artistic history. On the island, silver craftsmanship has a long history. Balinese artisans are renowned for their top-notch craftsmanship, intricate patterns, and meticulous attention to detail. As you visit the nearby markets and shops, you'll be mesmerised by the wide variety of silver jewellery on display.

One of the most popular types of silver jewellery in Bali is traditional Balinese filigree jewellery.

Filigree is made by patiently weaving and twisting thin silver wires into complex designs and patterns. The result is a wonderfully intricate piece of jewellery that showcases the skill and workmanship of Balinese master craftsmen. You may choose from a variety of filigree designs, like earrings, necklaces, bracelets, and rings.

In addition to its filigree, Bali is also known for its silver jewellery set with semi-precious stones. The beautiful contrast produced by the combination of sparkling silver and vibrant gemstones lends a sense of refinement to any ensemble. A few examples of the gemstones that Balinese artists skillfully use into their works of art are amethyst, turquoise, and citrine. The result is stunning jewellery that is both visually pleasing and culturally significant.

Although silver jewellery predominates on the Bali market, gold jewellery is also highly valued by visitors. A large variety of designs and styles may be found in Bali's growing gold jewellery sector. From intricate Balinese-inspired motifs to clean and minimalist goods, every taste and style is catered to.

One of the distinguishing characteristics of Balinese gold jewellery is the use of traditional techniques like granulation and repoussé. By hammering it from the opposite side, gold is sculpted and embossed using the granulation and repoussé processes, respectively. Granulation is the process of melting tiny gold spheres onto a surface to create intricate designs. Balinese gold jewellery has a feeling of elegance and beauty because of these techniques, which have been passed down through the years.

Bali offers several jewellery stores and markets, particularly in popular tourist destinations like Ubud and Seminyak, which are great for travellers. These companies provide a wide assortment of silver and gold jewellery to accommodate all preferences and pricing points. It's a good idea to shop around, compare prices, and browse through different styles to make sure you get the perfect item that speaks to you.

It's crucial to buy jewellery in Bali from reputable vendors that provide genuine goods of the highest quality. Authenticity of the materials used should be questioned at respected, long-standing stores. Additionally, don't be scared to ask for reduced prices since haggling is common in local markets.

In conclusion, Bali will be a treasure trove for those shopping for silver and gold jewellery. The island is a jeweller's paradise because to its long creative history, skilled craftsmanship, and vast range of designs. Whether you're seeking a unique present or a stunning addition to your collection, Bali's jewellery scene offers a first-rate shopping experience. On your journey to the Island of the Gods, don't forget to take in the splendour of Bali's silver and gold jewellery.

## Balinese Painting

The captivating and bright art of Balinese painting captures the rich cultural legacy of the island of Bali. A wonderful method to immerse oneself in the creative traditions of the island and comprehend its cultural identity for visitors to Bali is to explore the world of Balinese painting. Balinese artwork delivers a visual feast that is likely to enthral art fans and curious tourists alike with its distinctive style, minute details, and brilliant colours.

Balinese art, which is rooted in religious and mythical themes, provides a visual account of the island's Hindu-Balinese beliefs. In addition to images from Balinese mythology and local tales, the paintings often include scenes from classical Hindu epics like the Ramayana and the Mahabharata. To depict these stories on canvas or paper, the artists combine traditional methods like the intricate and exquisite Kamasan style with the more modern Ubud style.

The exquisite attention to detail in Balinese paintings is one of its most remarkable features. Artists diligently work for hours to create complex patterns and motifs, often using delicate brushes made of animal hair. The paintings are distinguished by their complex compositions, which include several individuals, well rendered landscapes, and extravagant outfits. These minute details are evidence of the talent and commitment of Balinese artists, whose technique has been refined through many generations of creative practice.

The bright colour scheme of Balinese paintings is another noteworthy aspect. To make their creations come to life, the painters utilise strong, vibrant colours. The paintings' vibrant hues of red, yellow, green, and blue take centre stage, producing a spectacular visual impression. In addition to being aesthetically pleasing, the usage of such brilliant hues also symbolises the island's dynamic and colourful culture.

While current painters are exploring new forms and subjects while fusing traditional methods with contemporary influences, Balinese painting has its origins in ancient traditions. A strong modern art scene has emerged in Bali as a result of the blending of the old and the new, with galleries and studios presenting a wide variety of creative styles.

There are many options for tourists who want to learn more about Balinese art. Balinese paintings from both the traditional and modern periods are available in curated collections in art galleries and museums across Bali, especially in the cultural centre of Ubud. These exhibits provide a thorough overview of the many topics, methods, and styles used in Balinese art.

Visitors may also get a first-hand look at the creative process by going to art studios and workshops. They may see painters at work, learn about their methods, and even give painting a go with the help of qualified teachers. Travellers may interact with the creative process and have a greater understanding of the expertise and artistry that go into Balinese painting via such immersive encounters.

Balinese painting is an alluring art form that provides a glimpse into Bali's cultural history and aesthetic traditions. Visitors get the chance to discover the island's creative environment and its distinctive combination of history and modernity thanks to its detailed details, vivid colours, and fascinating storylines. The beauty and originality of Balinese painting is guaranteed to excite visitors to Bali, whether they want to see works in galleries, tour artists' studios, or even produce their own masterpiece.

## Traditional Dance and Music

If you want to enjoy a really authentic cultural experience, explore Bali's rich creative past via its traditional performing arts. Whether it's the throbbing beats of the gamelan orchestra or the graceful movements of the Balinese dancers, the island is a fascinating display of talent and beauty.

The heart of Balinese traditional performing arts is the gamelan, a collection of musical instruments that produces mesmerising tunes. The sound produced by the gamelan, which primarily uses metallophones, gongs, and drums, is distinctive and recognisable. The intricate and symphonic music played by talented musicians promotes serenity and a sense of spiritual connection. An integral part of Balinese culture, the gamelan is often performed with traditional dances during temple rites, regal processions, and traditional performances.

In terms of traditional dances, Bali is home to a vast range of dance forms that illustrate mythology and historical events. Instead of being mere exhibitions, the dances are revered as sacred events that commemorate the island's spiritual beliefs. One of the most well-known dances, the Legong, is defined by its intricate and delicate movements. This dance is performed by young girls dressed in vibrant clothes, showcasing their grace and agility as they go. Another well-liked dance genre is the Barong, a dramatic and mystical performance that depicts the continuous struggle between good and evil.

Due to the fact that each village in Bali has its own unique dance and music traditions, visitors may see a broad range of artistic manifestations there. Whether you go to Ubud, which is regarded as the cultural hub of Bali, or you visit rural areas, you will certainly encounter captivating performances that will capture you. The Balinese people take great pride in their cultural heritage and are always happy to share their rituals with visitors, making it a wonderfully immersive and fascinating experience.

Experiencing a traditional dance performance in Bali is a sensory-rich experience. The dancers' vivid costumes, beautiful makeup, and deft hand gestures make for an amazing spectacle. The accompanying music, played expertly by the gamelan ensemble, transports you to another world. The artists fascinate the audience with their expressive facial expressions and dance narratives that depict a range of emotions, from joy and love to fury and despair.

Anyone interested in learning more about Balinese arts may take courses at a number of cultural and educational institutes. These provide the ability to learn the fundamentals of dance, appreciate the value of wearing traditional clothing, and even experiment with gamelan instruments. Such in-depth interactions enhance your understanding of the culture while also fostering a greater regard for the dedication and ability required to master these art forms.

Last but not least, Bali's traditional dance and music provide guests a unique opportunity to take in the island's rich cultural heritage. The mesmerising movements of the Balinese dancers and the captivating tunes of the gamelan orchestra combine to produce an unforgettable experience. By learning about the many dance forms and seeing performances in various villages, travellers may get a glimpse of the Balinese people's artistic expression and spiritual depth. So embrace the allure of Bali's traditional dance and music and let it transport you into a realm of beauty and spirituality.

# Chapter 8. Gastronomy and Local Cuisine

## *Balinese Cuisine Overview*

Balinese food, which combines flavorful spices, seasonal ingredients, and traditional cooking methods, is an authentic representation of the island's rich cultural past. It is essential for visitors to Bali to experience the native cuisine. To assist you explore the gastronomic pleasures of this tropical paradise, here is an introduction of Balinese cuisine.

In Bali, rice, sometimes referred to as "nasi," is the main component of practically all meals. Nasi goreng, a fragrant fried rice meal prepared with spices, veggies, and your choice of meat or fish, is one of the most well-known Balinese cuisines. Nasi campur, which consists of steamed rice served with a variety of tiny amounts of meat, veggies, and sambal (a spicy sauce), is another well-known rice-based meal.

Balinese cuisine heavily relies on spices, which give the foods their distinctive tastes. The traditional spice paste known as bumbu is made out of a mixture of shrimp paste, shallots, garlic, chile, ginger, and turmeric. Many Balinese recipes, such as the well-known babi guling (suckling pig) and ayam betutu (spiced roast chicken), start with this pungent paste.

Bali offers a broad variety of seafood selections for foodies. Popular options include grilled fish, calamari, prawns, and clams. Fresh seafood eateries can be found in abundance at Jimbaran Bay, where you may have a delectable seafood feast while taking in the beautiful sunset.

Bali has a wide variety of plant-based choices for those looking for a vegetarian or vegan experience. It is simple to discover a range of nutritious and delicious vegetarian recipes on the island thanks to the rich soil that generates an abundance of fruits and vegetables. There is something for every pallet, from tempeh and tofu-based foods to gado-gado (vegetable salad with peanut sauce).

The renowned satay must be mentioned while discussing Balinese food. Meat is skewered and grilled for satay, which is often served with a peanut sauce, rice cakes, and seasonal vegetables. Popular options include the flavour-packed chicken satay (sate ayam) and pork satay (sate babi).

Visit the neighbourhood warungs (small restaurants) and night markets to really sample Balinese cuisine. You may enjoy a variety of local snacks and street cuisine at this location, including bakso (meatball soup), pisang goreng (fried bananas), and martabak (stuffed pancake). These affordable choices give a genuine flavour of Balinese food as well as a chance to socialise with the locals.

Don't pass up Bali's delicious desserts if you have a sweet taste. A well-liked option is bubur injin, a black rice pudding made with coconut milk. Other sweet delights include klepon (glutinous rice balls filled with palm sugar), dadar gulung (coconut-stuffed pancake), and pisang rai (banana wrapped in sticky rice).

Try some of the local libations with your lunch. A cup of the rich, fragrant Balinese coffee, which is famed for being produced in Bali, is a must-try. If you want something cool to drink, get a fresh young coconut or try the well-liked local beverage jamu, which is a herbal mixture said to have health advantages.

Balinese food is a delicious fusion of tastes, textures, and spices that will tempt your palate. Bali provides a gastronomic experience unlike any other, with everything from delightful rice dishes to luscious grilled meats, from fresh seafood to delicious vegetarian alternatives, and from street cuisine to decadent sweets. Discovering the many tastes and distinctive cuisines that are firmly anchored in Balinese culture and history makes exploring the local culinary scene in and of itself an experience.

Attending a traditional Balinese cooking lesson is among the greatest ways to enjoy Balinese food. These courses provide an immersive learning environment where you can discover the methods and insider tips for making genuine Balinese cuisine. These lessons provide a practical chance to dig further into the nuances of Balinese cuisine, from purchasing goods from neighbourhood markets to mastering the art of spice mixing.

Balinese food is renowned for its aesthetic presentation as well as its robust tastes. Balinese chefs take great delight in producing meals that are a feast for the eyes as well as the palate. Every dish is an artistic creation that showcases the lively culture of the island, from the deft fruit carvings to the brilliant combinations of spices and sauces.

It's crucial to accept the idea of "nasi campur," or mixed rice, while eating in Bali. This gives you a chance to try a range of meals at once and gives you a genuine experience of the regional cuisine. Many restaurants and warungs serve nasi campur in a buffet manner, allowing you to pick from a variety of foods to assemble your own unique meal.

It should be noted that the cuisine of the island of Bali might differ somewhat from area to region. The hilly districts provide robust cuisine crafted with regional ingredients, while the coastal regions, like Jimbaran and Sanur, are well renowned for their fresh seafood specialties. You'll get the opportunity to sample the distinctive tastes and delicacies that each area of Bali has to offer by touring its many regions.

Lastly, it's crucial to respect regional traditions and manners while savouring Bali's gastronomic delicacies. The friendliness of Balinese people is renowned, as is their reverence for cuisine. Spend some time enjoying each meal, conversing with the people, and expressing your gratitude for the tastes and labours that went into making the food.

Finally, the food scene in Bali is a vivacious tapestry of tastes, spices, and cultural influences. Balinese cuisine will definitely create a lasting impression, whether you're a food connoisseur or just wanting to indulge in new culinary experiences. So start your culinary trip and let Bali's alluring tastes transport you on a voyage of pleasure and joy.

## Popular Balinese Dishes

Balinese food is a harmonic fusion of flavorful spices, fresh ingredients, and rich tastes, creating meals that are a genuine joy for the palate. If you're thinking of visiting Bali, be sure to try these well-known Balinese delicacies, which will elevate your dining experience.

Babi Guling is a meal that you must have when visiting Bali. It is a flavorful roasted suckling pig that has been marinated with a mixture of chilli, garlic, turmeric, and other spices. The pig is perfectly slow-roasted, producing flesh that is tender and skin that is crunchy. Steamed rice, lawar (a combination of veggies, coconut, and minced meat), and sambal (a hot chilli paste) are often served with babi guling.

2. Nasi Goreng: Popular across Indonesia, especially Bali, nasi goreng is a fried rice dish. Precooked rice is stir-fried with a variety of veggies, shrimp, chicken, and seasonings including garlic, soy sauce, and chilli. Frequent accompaniments for nasi goreng include pickles, shrimp crackers, and a fried egg on top.

3. Sate Lilit: Made from minced chicken, pig, or fish, sate lilit is a typical Balinese satay. Before being impaled onto lemongrass sticks, the meat is combined with grated coconut, herbs, and spices. After that, it is roasted over charcoal, producing a meal that is aromatic and flavorful.

Steamed rice and a serving of sambal are the usual accompaniments to sate lilit.

4. Ayam Betutu: A typical Balinese meal, ayam betutu is a whole chicken marinated in a blend of spices, including turmeric, ginger, garlic, chilli, and lemongrass. After that, the chicken is wrapped in banana leaves and cooked slowly for a number of hours to enable the flavours to permeate the flesh. The outcome is chicken that is extraordinarily tasty, fragrant, and soft. Typically, lawar, sambal, and steamed rice are served with ayam betutu.

5. Bebek Betutu: This dish is similar to Ayam Betutu but uses duck as the primary component instead of chicken. Similar techniques are used to make the duck, which is wrapped in banana leaves, marinated in spices, and cooked slowly. The meat develops a deep, spicy taste and becomes very soft and juicy. Steamed rice, sambal, and fresh veggies are typical accompaniments to bebek betutu dishes.

6. Lawar: A common side dish or companion to the main course in Balinese cuisine is the traditional salad known as lawar. It is a concoction of minced meat (typically pig or chicken), spices, and finely chopped veggies. Lawar is available in a variety of colours, including white, red, and green, each with a unique blend of ingredients. It adds a crisp and energising edge to the dish.

7. Bubur Sumsum: If you have a sweet craving, you should try this well-liked Balinese dish. It is a warm, creamy rice pudding prepared with pandan leaves, coconut milk, and rice flour. Typically, bubur sumsum is topped with shredded coconut and served with palm sugar syrup. It delivers a wonderful fusion of tastes and textures.

These are just a handful of the mouthwatering Balinese foods you may enjoy when visiting Bali 8. Gado-Gado: The well-known Indonesian salad gado-gado is also well-liked in Bali. It is a mix of steamed vegetables with a peanut sauce dressing, including spinach, bean sprouts, cabbage, and cucumber. Boiling eggs, tofu, and tempeh are often served with gado-gado. With the addition of the peanut sauce, this meal gives the ideal harmony of tastes and textures.

9. Sate Babi: Pork satay, also known as sate babi, is a popular street meal in Bali. It is made up of tiny slices of marinated pork that are skewered onto bamboo sticks and cooked over an open flame. The pork is given a delicious and somewhat sweet taste by marinating it in a combination of soy sauce, garlic, ginger, and other spices. Normally, rice cakes and peanut sauce are included with sate babi.

10. Lawar Kuwir: A special Balinese cuisine, Lawar Kuwir combines shredded coconut, minced beef, and other herbs and spices. Fresh blood, often from pigs or ducks, is what distinguishes it and gives it a unique flavor and texture. A complicated, flavorful meal called Lawar Kuwir is often served during important events and festivities.

11. Pepes Ikan: Fish is marinated in a fiery concoction of herbs, spices, and lime juice in this traditional Balinese meal. To let the spices permeate the fish, the marinated fish is then wrapped in banana leaves and steamed or grilled. The outcome is a meal that is delicate, aromatic, and somewhat smoky thanks to the banana leaves. Steamed rice and sambal are often served with pepes ikan.

12. Jaje Bali: Various traditional Balinese sweets are referred to as "jaje Bali" and are often eaten during religious rituals and other special occasions. The sizes, tastes, and forms of these delectable delights vary. Popular examples are Bubur Injin (black glutinous rice porridge with coconut milk and palm sugar), Dadar Gulung (pandan crepes filled with shredded coconut and palm sugar), and Klepon (rice flour balls filled with palm sugar and covered in grated coconut). A delicious method to digest food and experience the sweet side of Balinese cuisine is to visit Jaje Bali.

Don't pass up the chance to taste this well-known Balinese cuisine while in Bali. Whether you like hot tastes, fragrant herbs, or unusual combinations, Bali's culinary pleasures will leave you wanting more. Accept the regional tastes, savour the traditional meals, and allow Balinese cuisine to take your taste buds on a trip they won't soon forget.

## *Restaurants and Warungs*

The energetic food scene in Bali offers a heap of choices, from upscale cafés to humble warungs, where voyagers can set out on a wonderful culinary experience. Bali has everything, from traditional Balinese cuisine to international cuisine.

Bali's restaurants offer a wide range of international cuisines to satisfy a variety of palates. There are a lot of fine dining establishments in popular tourist destinations like Kuta, Ubud, and Seminyak that offer exquisite menus created by talented chefs. Combining traditional Balinese ingredients with international cooking techniques, these restaurants showcase a fusion of international culinary influences. The variety of choices, ranging from Mediterranean to Asian fusion, ensures that tourists will have an unforgettable dining experience.

Warungs are the best option for travellers who want to get a feel for the local culture. These little, family-possessed diners are dissipated across the island, offering genuine Balinese cooking at reasonable costs. Warungs are known for their customary dishes like nasi goreng (broiled rice), mie goreng (seared noodles), and satay (barbecued sticks). Travellers can get a real taste of Bali's culinary history by tasting these delicious treats, which are made with fresh ingredients and traditional recipes that have been passed down through the generations.

The opportunity to dine like a local is one of the unique features of warungs. Warungs offer an authentic and immersive dining experience due to their relaxed and casual atmosphere. Locals often talk, savour their meals, and tell stories over a cup of fragrant Balinese coffee or a cool young coconut. The cordial and inviting nature of the warung proprietors adds an additional appeal to the eating experience, making it a noteworthy experience for explorers looking for a sample of nearby culture.

Be sure to explore Bali beyond the popular tourist attractions to discover hidden gems. In the open country, you'll find warungs set against amazing scenes, encompassed by lavish rice patios or ignoring beautiful sea shores. Travellers can savour authentic Balinese cuisine at these off-the-beaten-path dining establishments while taking in the island's stunning natural beauty.

Bali's restaurant scene meets a variety of requirements, including those with dietary restrictions and those looking for healthier options. The island brags an overflow of veggie lover and vegetarian amicable foundations, as well as eateries having some expertise in natural and privately obtained fixings. Additionally, many establishments offer dairy-free and gluten-free options, allowing travellers with special dietary requirements to still enjoy Bali's vibrant flavours.

Don't miss out on the chance to look around at the local markets if you want to fully experience Bali's culinary offerings. Customary business sectors, for example, Pasar Badung in Denpasar or Ubud Market are mother lodes of new produce, flavours, and nearby tidbits. These markets give you a glimpse into Balinese culture and let you try delicious street foods like bubur sumsum (rice flour porridge) and pisang goreng (fried bananas). Travellers can interact with the locals, learn about traditional ingredients, and even take cooking classes as part of this immersive experience.

In conclusion, tourists can enjoy a delightful culinary journey in Bali's restaurants and warungs. The island caters to all tastes, whether you're looking for fine dining or authentic Balinese cuisine. From upscale foundations serving combination dishes to humble warungs concealed in quiet corners, Bali welcomes you to investigate its different flavours and drench yourself in its rich culinary legacy. So, bring your appetite and get ready for a culinary adventure in Bali, a tropical paradise.

# Chapter 9. Shopping and Markets

## *Ubud Art Market*

Ubud is a thriving town in the centre of Bali, Indonesia, that is famous for its beautiful landscapes, lively art scene, and extensive cultural heritage. Among the many tourist attractions, the Ubud Art Market stands out as a must-visit location. This bustling market in the centre of town, which is also a treasure trove for those looking for one-of-a-kind souvenirs and handicrafts, is a great place to learn more about the island's artistic traditions.

In the nearby language, the Ubud Workmanship Market is otherwise called "Pasar Seni Ubud," and it is an energetic market that grandstands the expertise and creativity of Balinese craftsmans. From intricately cut woodwork to energetic materials, flawless silver gems, hand-painted batik clothing, and captivating Balinese compositions, you can find a different group of traditional specialties here. The market is a haven for art enthusiasts, art collectors, and those curious about the island's cultural past.

One of the most appealing aspects of the Ubud Art Market is the opportunity to interact directly with local artisans and artists. It is a wellspring of extraordinary pride for the overwhelming majority of the merchants, a considerable lot of whom are themselves craftsmans, to make sense of the narratives and strategies behind their manifestations. Visitors can observe the creation of these masterpieces and gain a deeper understanding of the skills that have been passed down through time.

You'll be greeted by a rainbow of colours and sounds as you wander the narrow back streets of the market. The enthusiastic air is updated by the soothing smiles and very much arranged trade of the merchants, making an energetic and inviting temperament. Because no one really knows what unlikely treasures you might stumble across, conducting an investigation into the market is an undertaking in and of itself.

In addition to its artistic offerings, the Ubud Art Market is an excellent location to experience the essence of Balinese daily life. The market attracts locals as well as tourists for the purpose of purchasing necessities. Watching the locals bargain for fresh produce, spices, and textiles provides an authentic glimpse into the island's vibrant culture and traditions.

When you go to the Ubud Workmanship Market, it's important to get better at dealing. In addition to being expected, bargaining is a necessary part of shopping. The fervour of the experience is increased by the way that sellers commonly start with more exorbitant costs. As the Balinese people value kindness and generosity, make sure to approach the cycle with joy and respect.

Have some time off from the clamouring market and investigate the encompassing region after an elating shopping binge. Ubud is so popular because of its serene landscapes, lush rice terraces, and beautiful temples. Within walking distance of the market, you can find hidden gems like the well-known Monkey Forest, where you can interact with jovial macaques in the middle of a sacred sanctuary.

In conclusion, the vibrant atmosphere, cultural immersion, and artistic excellence of the Ubud Art Market are all captivating. This market is a must-see if you're a craft enthusiast, a treasure hunter, or just an explorer looking for a real experience. By immersing yourself in the hues, textures, and tales that make Bali's artistic heritage so captivating, you can take a piece of this magical island home with you.

## Sukawati Art Market

Sukawati Art Market has a well established history that traces all the way back to the 1980s when it previously earned respect as a centre point for conventional Balinese expressions and specialties. The market, which is in the Gianyar Regency and is only a short drive from Ubud, has come to be associated with the island's artistic heritage. It is a treasure trove of Balinese art and culture because local artisans from surrounding villages gather here to display and sell their handmade creations.

Creative Fortunes and Legitimate Gifts:
Traditional paintings, wood carvings, textiles, silverware, and intricate handmade jewellery are just a few of the many artistic treasures that can be found at this market. The complicated wood carvings found in Sukawati Workmanship Market portray Balinese old stories, fanciful animals, and scenes from regular day to day existence, displaying the remarkable craftsmanship of the neighbourhood craftsmans. Traditional paintings depicting Bali's landscapes, vibrant ceremonies, and religious themes are also available to visitors.

The market has a wide range of batik fabrics, intricately woven songket, and traditional ikat textiles for those who are interested in textiles. These exquisite pieces, which are frequently utilised in traditional ceremonies, can bring a little bit of Bali's rich culture into your home decor. Additionally, the market features a selection of jewellery and silverware with traditional Balinese designs, making it possible to acquire authentic and one-of-a-kind keepsakes.

Getting Around the Market:
The Sukawati Art Market can be a thrilling experience, but there are a few things to keep in mind. There are several sections of the market, each of which focuses on a different kind of art and crafts. Take as much time as necessary to investigate each part, wrangle with the sellers, and contrast costs with guarantee you get the best incentive for your cash. Haggling is a typical practice here, so make it a point to arrange the cost, however make sure to do as such with deference and a grin.

Additionally, it's a good idea to get to the market early to avoid the crowds and enjoy a more leisurely shopping experience. The market can get crowded later in the day because it draws a steady stream of tourists. As the majority of vendors prefer cash transactions over credit cards, don't forget to bring cash.

Getting to know the culture:
Sukawati Art Market provides a chance to immerse yourself in the vibrant Balinese culture in addition to its commercial aspect. Engage with the local artisans, gain insight into their creative processes, and learn about the stories that go along with the masterpieces they create. Large numbers of the merchants are glad to share their insight and energy for Balinese workmanship, permitting you to develop your appreciation for their art.

Additionally, Sukawati Art Market gives visitors a glimpse into the island's performing arts scene by hosting live performances of traditional Balinese music and dance at specific times.

During your visit, don't miss the chance to see a captivating cultural performance.

In conclusion, visitors looking for a true taste of Bali's art and culture should not miss Sukawati Art Market. With its huge range of imaginative fortunes, enthusiastic air, and potential open doors for social drenching, the market offers a significant excursion through the innovative soul of the island. Therefore, plan some time to explore during your trip to Bali.

## *Kuta Beachwalk*

Kuta Beachwalk is the place to go if you're thinking about taking a trip to Indonesia's picturesque island of Bali and want to shop till you drop. Kuta, one of the main tourist locations on the island, is home to the enormous shopping and entertainment complex Kuta Beachwalk, which offers customers an unmatched shopping experience.

As soon as you reach Kuta Beachwalk, you'll be greeted with a lively atmosphere, with crowded cafés and shops along the pedestrian-friendly pathways. The architecture of the complex demonstrates a subtle blending of modern and traditional Balinese design, creating a unique and welcoming ambiance. Whether you're a gourmet, a shopaholic, or simply interested in experiencing the local culture, Kuta Beachwalk has something to offer everyone.

A great area to shop is Kuta Beachwalk. The complex is home to a wide range of domestic and foreign enterprises, including posh clothes boutiques and unique gift shops. Everything is offered, including handmade items, classic Balinese art, and stylish clothing and accessories. Browse the numerous shops at your leisure; friendly and helpful personnel are standing by to assist you in choosing the best memento to remember your trip to Bali.

After engaging in some retail therapy, you may satisfy your hunger at one of the many restaurants and cafés in Kuta Beachwalk. From local delicacies to other countries' cuisines, the dining options are diverse and pleasing to all palates. Between shopping expeditions, grab a quick snack to keep you going, or have a leisurely dinner while taking in the spectacular coastline views. Bali's reputation as a foodie's paradise is evident in the variety of foods available in Kuta Beachwalk.

Along with dining and shopping, Kuta Beachwalk also offers a range of entertainment options. Watch the newest blockbuster at the cinema, or check out live performances by artists from other cultures on the outdoor stage. The complex often supports shows and activities that promote Bali's extensive cultural heritage. It's the perfect place to get fully immersed in the vibrant local arts scene and experience the creative ambiance of the island.

When you need a break from shopping and entertainment, Kuta Beachwalk provides a tranquil sanctuary close to the beach. Enjoy the sunlight while strolling along the sandy beaches or cool yourself in the clear waters of the Indian Ocean. At the beach, surfers often assemble, so if you're feeling brave, you may rent a board and ride the waves. Kuta Beachwalk offers the best of both worlds, whether you're seeking adventure or relaxation.

In conclusion, everyone travelling to Bali should include a stop to Kuta Beachwalk on their agenda. With its vibrant atmosphere, a large range of shopping options, delectable culinary options, and magnificent coastal backdrop, it undoubtedly has something to offer everyone. Whether you want to shop 'til you drop, taste in scrumptious cuisine, or simply take in the laid-back island vibe, Kuta Beachwalk ensures a fantastic experience. So prepare for a shopping extravaganza near Bali's stunning beaches by gathering your possessions, getting some sunscreen, and packing light.

## Seminyak Square

Seminyak Square is a bustling hub with a range of activities for travellers searching for a memorable vacation, and it is situated in the heart of Bali's well-known Seminyak beach resort zone. Due to its collection of opulent shops, stylish cafés, lively bars, and historical landmarks, Seminyak Square is a must-see spot for tourists visiting the enchanting island of Bali.

They will be in a shoppers' paradise as they navigate the maze of fashion boutiques, galleries, and designer shops that make up Seminyak Square. This shopping paradise has something for everyone, from well-known local brands to renowned worldwide fashion firms, and there is something here for any budget. If you're looking for fashionable clothing, one-of-a-kind crafts, or priceless jewels, Seminyak Square is the place to go. After a fruitful shopping excursion, relax and rejuvenate at one of the luxury spas in the area.

Foodies will be delighted by the extensive selection of culinary choices available in Seminyak Square. On the plaza, there are several restaurants serving both regional and international cuisines. Every taste is catered to with meals including authentic Indonesian food, tantalising seafood, fusion cuisine, and gourmet delights. Take it easy over supper at a cosy café or treat yourself to fine dining at one of the area's exclusive eateries. After that, unwind with a refreshing beverage at one of the fun beach clubs or bars, where you can dance the night away or sway to live music.

Seminyak Square is a cultural hub in addition to a location to dine and shop. A short distance from the square sits the Pura Petitenget Temple, a famed Balinese Hindu temple known for its ornate architecture and ceremonial practices. The colourful local culture is completely accessible to tourists, who may also see locals performing traditional rituals and dances. A short distance from Seminyak Square lies Petitenget Beach, where you may relax in the sun, cool off in the blue waters, or enjoy a leisurely stroll along the sandy shore.

Those seeking a more laid-back experience may choose from a variety of spa and relaxation services at Seminyak Square. Many yoga studios and wellness centres provide a tranquil environment for holistic health treatments, yoga instruction, and meditation. Go for a calming spa treatment, practice mindfulness, or attend a yoga retreat to rejuvenate your body and mind.

Seminyak Square is an excellent place to begin exploring other Bali attractions due to its central location. The majestic Tanah Lot Temple is only a short drive away; it is perched on a rocky outcropping and provides breathtaking views of the Indian Ocean. Visit Ubud, a nearby town renowned for its lush rice terraces, art galleries, and traditional crafts, as an alternative.

In conclusion, Seminyak Square is a busy area that offers tourists visiting Bali a wide range of activities. Whether you're searching for retail therapy, delectable cuisine, cultural immersion, relaxation, or adventure, Seminyak Square has it all. Explore Bali's enchanted locale, look for undiscovered treasures, and create lifetime memories.

## Beach Street Markets

One of the many attractions that tourists looking for a true local experience shouldn't miss are the Beach Street Markets. These markets, which are found in Bali's city centre, draw visitors from all over the world because of their remarkable blend of art, culture, and mouthwatering food.

The Beach Street Markets are a hive of activity where regional entrepreneurs and artisans showcase their talent and creativity. These markets, which are hidden along the shore, provide a range of homemade items, jewellery, clothing, and artwork. By browsing the booths, visitors may discover one-of-a-kind souvenirs to remember their trip or unique gifts to bring back home.

One of the main attractions of the Beach Street Markets is the opportunity to socialise with the locals. The hospitable vendors are always eager to discuss their artistic creations, the cultural significance attached to them, and the processes used to create them. This interaction is advantageous for tourists since it enlightens them about the island's traditions and the care that goes into each product.

For food aficionados, the markets, which provide a tantalising range of treats from all across Bali, are a haven. With choices ranging from elegant cafés offering fusion cuisine to street food sellers selling enticing local delicacies, visitors may go on a culinary journey unlike any other. The enticing aroma of freshly cooked satay, nasi goreng, and sate lilit draws tourists to indulge in Bali's flourishing cuisine industry.

The regular live performances by local musicians and dancers at the Beach Street Markets provide another level of enjoyment. The atmosphere is filled with traditional Balinese music, and skilled dancers show their graceful movements, transporting visitors to a wonderful world where they may completely immerse themselves in the culture. Visitors may enjoy the upbeat music, join in the festivities, and create lifetime memories.

Along with a vast range of artistic and gastronomic delights, the Beach Street Markets are a terrific place to unwind and relax. Since the resort is adjacent to Bali's stunning beaches, guests may take a break from their shopping spree and unwind in the sun while listening to the relaxing sound of crashing waves. Tourists may rejuvenate their spirits in the tranquil atmosphere offered by the vibrant ocean colours and the smooth sand before continuing their exploration of the markets.

If visitors want a more in-depth experience, the Beach Street Markets often provide seminars and demonstrations where they may learn traditional skills like batik painting, wood carving, or Balinese dance. These hands-on encounters provide tourists the opportunity to learn more about the locals and to take a bit of Bali's artistic history with them when they go.

Finally, visitors could enjoy a very memorable time at Bali's Beach Street Markets. With its diverse fusion of art, culture, and delicious cuisine, this vibrant hub creates a captivating atmosphere that perfectly embodies the essence of Bali. Whether you're looking for one-of-a-kind souvenirs, craving exquisite cuisine, or just wishing to immerse yourself in the local culture, the Beach Street Markets are a must-visit venue that will leave you with precious memories of your time in Bali.

# Chapter 10. Outdoor Activities and Wellness

## *Yoga and Meditation Retreats*

Due to its serene environment and well rooted cultural traditions, Bali has become more popular among practitioners of yoga and meditation. The island is the ideal location for yoga and meditation retreats due to its unique blend of unrivalled natural beauty, vibrant spirituality, and top-notch wellness services.

These retreats are surrounded by some of Bali's various outdoor areas, which include beautiful beaches, lush rice terraces, and dense rainforests. Yoga and meditation in the midst of nature may enhance the whole experience by allowing guests to connect with their inner selves while taking in Bali's tranquil surroundings.

For persons of all skill levels, from novices to seasoned practitioners, the island offers a broad variety of retreat options. Numerous spas, lodging establishments, and retreat centres in Bali provide comprehensive programs that combine holistic treatment, mindfulness, and cultural immersion with yoga and meditation practices. Throughout these retreats, skilled instructors and facilitators guide participants on a transformative journey of self-discovery and rejuvenation.

One of the primary advantages of outdoor retreats in Bali is the opportunity to practise yoga and meditation in a range of stunning settings. Imagine doing yoga while the sound of the waves crashing is soothingly audible under your feet. Or visualise yourself meditating while surrounded by Bali's verdant rice terraces, the vibrant colours of the surroundings, and the gentle rustling of swaying palm trees. Such serene outdoor locations provide visitors a chance to relax, re-establish touch with nature, and find inner peace.

Along with the physical and emotional benefits, Bali yoga and meditation retreats provide a window to Balinese spirituality and culture. Every facet of daily life in Bali is infused with traditions and rituals, and these retreats often include elements of Balinese mysticism including temple visits, purification rituals, and Western medical treatments. As a result, participants may forge deep connections with the community and learn more about the island's fascinating cultural history.

Bali has a vibrant wellness culture outside of the retreat facilities itself. Numerous holistic spas, vegan and vegetarian restaurants, and health-conscious cafés that provide a variety of wellness services and nutritious cuisine can be found on the island. Travellers may add healthy meals, soothing massages, and other rejuvenating activities to their yoga and meditation routines to further enhance their overall wellness.

Additionally, Bali's comfortable climate enables year-round access to outdoor retreats for yoga and meditation. The island's tropical setting, which has comfortable temperatures and plenty of sunshine, is ideal for outdoor activities. Whether it's a morning yoga session by the beach or a sunset meditation in a lovely garden, the island's ambiance enhances the whole experience by creating a sense of tranquillity and vitality.

As a result of its seductive natural landscapes, rich cultural past, and commitment to wellness, Bali is the ideal site for yoga and meditation retreats. Thanks to the island's outdoor yoga and meditation programs, visitors have a unique opportunity to embark on a thorough journey of self-discovery, health, and spiritual growth. Whether you are a beginner looking to learn more about these disciplines or an experienced yogi looking to improve your practice, Bali offers a variety of retreats that are certain to leave you feeling renewed, inspired, and connected to your inner self in the middle of the island's picturesque surroundings.

## *Balinese Spa and Wellness Centers*

In the midst of the breathtaking magnificence of this tropical environment, Balinese spa and wellness facilities stand out as popular outdoor pursuits for visitors seeking relaxation, regeneration, and a greater connection with themselves. These facilities combine traditional Balinese healing techniques, exotic natural ingredients, and serene outdoor settings to provide a full experience that restores the mind, body, and soul.

Balinese spas and wellness centres are thoughtfully designed to provide a peaceful environment where visitors may escape the bustle of everyday life. Since these institutions are surrounded by lush greenery, tranquil gardens, and cascading waterfalls, treatment and environment are seamlessly combined. The calming sound of flowing water, the perfume of lovely flowers, and the warm tropical breeze bring clients into a state of relaxation even before their treatment even begins.

Balinese spas and wellness centres are notable for their commitment to sustaining Bali's age-old healing traditions. The island has a long tradition of using holistic practices including massage treatment, body exfoliation, herbal baths, and meditation techniques. These traditions have been passed down through time and are now followed in order to promote peace and harmony on a greater scale. Visitors get the opportunity to experience the therapeutic benefits of Balinese treatments, which combine deep tissue massage, acupressure, and stretching to reduce stress, improve circulation, and restore energy flow.

Balinese spa and health centres also provide a range of treatments that are tailored to the needs and preferences of each customer. Traditional Balinese massages, lavish facials, hot stone therapies, and aromatherapy treatments are all available. Skilled therapists with a profound understanding of the body's energy systems and pressure points work their magic using organic oils, herbal mixtures, and exotic goods made from Bali's plentiful natural resources. These therapies not only revitalise the body but also encourage harmony and emotional tranquillity.

In addition to the therapeutic treatments, Balinese spas and wellness facilities often provide other amenities for complete relaxation and enjoyment. Many of them include yoga rooms, outdoor swimming pools, Jacuzzis, steam rooms, and other luxuries that allow visitors to unwind and discover their inner calm. Some establishments also provide yoga and meditation classes, allowing guests to experience the spiritual side of Balinese culture while taking in the breathtaking island surroundings.

Outdoor locations are common in Balinese spas and medical centres, which improves the experience. There are several structures located near to rice terraces, with views of lush valleys, or on serene beaches. In the outdoor pavilions and treatment rooms, visitors may completely immerse themselves in nature while breathing in the fresh air and admiring their surroundings. This blending of natural settings and healing practices creates a really transformative experience that leaves visitors feeling renewed and revitalised.

Visitors to Bali are required to partake in a Balinese spa and wellness treatment. It gives one the opportunity to get away from the tourist crowd and lose themselves in a serene, self-care, and holistic healing setting. Whether customers want a peaceful massage, a revitalising facial, or a rejuvenating yoga session, these facilities provide a place for rest and regeneration. Visitors have the opportunity to go on holistic self-discovery adventures among Bali's breathtaking natural settings at Balinese spas and wellness centres. They are more than just locations for outdoor recreation.

## Cycling and Trekking Tours

Cycling and hiking excursions in Bali are thrilling and engaging outdoor activities for those wishing to take in the natural beauty of the island. Due to its stunning environment, lush rice terraces, volcanic mountains, and vibrant culture, Bali is the ideal destination for anyone who wants to engage in these exhilarating activities. Whether you're an avid cyclist or an experienced trekker, Bali features a vast range of roads and routes that are ideal for all skill levels, making it a haven for outdoor enthusiasts.

Cycling excursions in Bali take you through stunning scenery and provide an up-close view of the lovely rural lifestyle on the island. A wonderful look into the way of life in the area is provided by cycling through charming villages, verdant rice fields, and traditional Balinese temples. You'll pass by waving children, friendly locals, and the tranquil sounds of nature as you cycle through the busy streets. The tour guides—often knowledgeable locals themselves—enhance your experience and improve your understanding of Balinese culture.

For those seeking a more challenging experience, mountain bike rides are also available, taking you off the beaten path and deep into Bali's countryside. You are nothing compared to the rush of adrenaline and sense of accomplishment you have while negotiating difficult terrain and dense forest. These walks reward you with breathtaking views of cascading waterfalls, soaring cliffs, and mountain temples at every turn.

Trekking excursions in Bali provide a range of pathways that emphasise the island's unique geography, making them enjoyable for both inexperienced and experienced hikers. Mount Batur, an active volcano renowned for its early-morning treks, is one of the most well-liked hiking locations. After climbing the mountain in the early morning darkness with the assistance of an experienced trekker, you'll be rewarded with a breathtaking sunrise that illuminates the surrounding mountains and the peaceful Lake Batur below.

Another worthwhile trekking option is to explore Bali's verdant forests and waterfalls. These trails lead you through lush foliage, over rivers, and up to jaw-dropping waterfalls nestled away in the tropical forest. The Tegalalang Rice Terraces are a well-liked tourist destination where visitors may meander among terraced rice fields, see the advanced irrigation systems, and interact with farmers as they tend to their crops.

Bali's cycling and hiking adventures are not only exhilarating journeys, but they also provide a sustainable way to visit the island. Visitors may lessen their carbon impact and engage with Bali's locals and natural environment by choosing these activities. Several tour operators give responsible tourism practises a high emphasis in order to make sure that the routes are ecologically sustainable and that the local communities profit from the rise in visitors.

As a result, cycling and hiking excursions in Bali provide tourists the opportunity to fully appreciate the island's appealing landscape, rich cultural past, and friendly locals. Outdoor pursuits like mountain biking across the countryside or trekking through rain forests and up mountains provide a unique perspective and a great experience. If you're planning a trip to Bali, be sure to organise cycling and trekking excursions so you can fully experience the island's natural beauty and create life-long memories.

## *Rafting and Canyoning Adventures*

Visitors to Bali may enjoy intriguing outdoor activities like rafting and canyoning trips, which provide a wonderful experience. The perfect location for these heart-pounding sports is Bali, which is famed for its stunning natural surroundings and many water sources. Whether you're an expert adventurer or a novice thrill seeker, rafting and canyoning in Bali are guaranteed to leave you with lifetime memories.

You'll have an amazing journey across Bali's pure rivers when rafting there, surrounded by the island's lush tropical woods and towering cliffs. The most popular rafting destination in Bali is the Ayung River, which is near to Ubud. As you navigate the river's rapids, you'll be mesmerised by the breathtaking scenery and the adrenaline rush of conquering the white water. The Ayung River offers a reasonable level of difficulty for both beginner and experienced rafters. A trained guide is present on every rafting expedition to ensure everyone's safety and to provide tips on how to have the best time possible.

Contrarily, canyoning allows you to see Bali's canyons' lesser-known attractions. You'll be swimming, climbing, scrambling, rappelling, and doing other activities as you navigate tight passages and tumbling waterfalls along the route. Two well-known canyoning spots in Bali, Gitgit and Kerenkali, provide thrilling descents that put your stamina and agility to the test. With the proper gear and under the guidance of experienced instructors, you'll have the opportunity to rappel down high cliffs, dive into natural pools, and down natural water slides. Canyoning in Bali provides a rare chance to see the island's untouched natural beauty firsthand.

Bali's rafting and canyoning adventures are accessible to a wide range of visitors since they can accommodate various levels of expertise. Bali offers something for everyone, whether you're a beginner seeking a water sport introduction or an experienced traveller looking for a new challenge. The activities are often organised by reputable adventure tour companies that prioritise safety and provide all necessary equipment.

Bali's rafting and canyoning adventures provide you the chance to fully appreciate the island's natural surroundings in addition to the thrill and adrenaline. While you paddle down the river or explore the canyons, you may take in Bali's lovely greenery, the sounds of nature, and the fresh air. These activities give you the chance to interact with the island more fully away from the congested tourist areas.

Many of Bali's rafting and canyoning excursions also include other activities for those seeking a full experience. Some journeys include pauses in traditional villages where you may see enduring customs and discover the way of life there. Others may provide you with a delicious lunch or beverages in the breathtaking surroundings after an adrenaline-fueled adventure, allowing you to relax and refresh.

Finally, Bali's canyoning and rafting adventures provide outdoor aficionados a once-in-a-lifetime experience. Bali is the perfect place to begin these thrilling activities due to its stunning environment, challenging water features, and knowledgeable operators. Rafting and canyoning in Bali are outdoor pursuits that, whether you're seeking an adrenaline rush, a connection with nature, or a combination of both, will leave you with lifelong memories of this magnificent island.

# Chapter 11. Festivals and Events

## *Galungan and Kuningan*

Among the various festivals conducted in Bali, Galungan and Kuningan stand out as two of the most prominent and anticipated events. These religious festivals showcase the island's deeply held spiritual convictions and provide guests seeking a genuine cultural encounter an unforgettable experience.

A celebration called Galungan celebrates the spirits of the dead and remembers when Dharma (good) triumphed over Adharma (evil). It is believed that during this ten-day celebration, the ghosts of ancestors descend to Earth to bless and bestow prosperity onto their descendants. Balinese residents meticulously wrap their homes, temples, and public areas with penjor, a tall, elaborately adorned bamboo pole that symbolises gratitude and riches, days before Galungan.

Galungan in Bali is a joyous time, and the festive atmosphere and eye-catching decorations will make you want to stay. The streets are animated with processions, traditional music, and dancing displays. The locals dress in their finest traditional garb, and it's common to see women delivering offerings to the temples while men fly kites to symbolise their contact with the heavens. A once-in-a-lifetime opportunity to see Balinese spiritual fervour and take part in their ceremonial rites is presented by visiting Bali's magnificent temples during Galungan, such as Besakih, Tanah Lot, or Uluwatu.

The festivities come to an end with Kuningan, which comes after Galungan. It is said that on this day, ancestral spirits who have travelled to Earth return to their heavenly residence. Kuningan's signature yellow presents are made with young coconut leaves, rice, and flowers. The Balinese believe that these sacrifices appease the spirits and ensure their safe ascent into the heavens.

During Kuningan, visitors may observe people dressed in yellow and the streets decked with yellow decorations. The atmosphere is one of cheerful celebration, with music, dancing, and traditional ceremonies taking place in temples all around the island. For those seeking a real experience, taking part in the offering-making process or joining a local family for a Kuningan feast gives a unique window into the Balinese way of life and their strong sense of community.

In addition to being religious events, Galungan and Kuningan provide an opportunity to study Bali's cultural past. Travellers may partake in a range of cultural activities, including seeing traditional dance performances, learning the art of offering, and taking cooking workshops where they can try authentic Balinese cuisine. By touring the local markets during these occasions, visitors may see the sale of colourful traditional crafts, attire, and delicacies.

Along with the festivities, Galungan and Kuningan provide a chance to take in Bali's breathtaking scenery. The island's breathtaking landscape is widely recognized, and during these celebrations, the vibrant gardens and emerald-green rice fields are at their most enticing. Visitors may take leisurely walks or bike rides in the countryside while admiring the breathtaking scenery and tranquillity that Bali is known for.

For those who want to explore the festival's spiritual aspect further, there are opportunities to engage with Balinese priests and spiritual authorities. They could provide prayers and blessings for the well-being of travellers as well as information on the rituals and traditions related to Galungan and Kuningan. This spiritual connection may have a profoundly calming and harmonious effect on visitors, which might be a really moving experience.

Two occasions when Bali's renowned hospitality is on full show are Galungan and Kuningan. Local families often invite visitors to join in the celebrations by opening their homes and hearts to share in the joy of the events. This is a unique chance to experience the genuine kindness and generosity of the Balinese people, forging ties and friendships that will be cherished long after the festivals have passed.

It's important to keep in mind that Kuningan and Galungan are based on the moon-centred Balinese calendar. Since the dates for these events often vary from year to year, it is a good idea to clarify the particular dates before making travel plans. The festivities often occur between February and August, but it's always a good idea to confirm the information with a reliable source or get in contact with the local tourism office.

Finally, Galungan and Kuningan are distinctive festivals that showcase Bali's rich spiritual heritage and cultural variety. These celebrations provide a unique opportunity for travellers seeking a fully immersed cultural experience to see traditional rites, take part in joyous festivities, admire Bali's breathtaking natural beauty, and get to know the friendly Balinese people. During this time of year, the island comes to life with colour, music, and an intense sense of devotion. By participating in Galungan and Kuningan, tourists may create lifelong memories and get a deeper understanding of Bali's fascinating culture.

## Nyepi (Balinese New Year)

Nyepi, also known as the Balinese New Year or the Day of Silence, is a unique and fascinating celebration that visitors to Bali should take part in. This biennial event is deeply rooted in Bali's culture and offers a fascinating window into the traditions and values of the island. Nyepi is a time of reflection, purification, and spiritual renewal, making it the ideal season for travellers seeking a tranquil and satisfying experience.

The Nyepi festival is celebrated in accordance with the Balinese Saka calendar, which starts on the first day of the new year. It usually takes place in March or April, depending on the lunar cycle. The island is characterised by a multitude of customs and rituals called Nyepi, which lasts for 24 hours and encourages reflection.

The peak of Nyepi is the day of absolute silence. The whole island comes to a complete standstill with no movement or noise permitted. It is forbidden to use electricity, make a fire, work, or even leave one's home or hotel. Visitors are advised to respect and participate in this unique tradition by staying in their accommodations and being silent. Although it could seem restricting, this is an unparalleled opportunity for reflection and refreshment.

In the days leading up to Nyepi, Bali comes alive with joyous events. Parades of colourful "ogoh-ogoh" effigies are held to honour the "Pengerupukan," or eve of Nyepi. These massive, demonic structures, created by local groups, are symbols of evil spirits. The energetic and vibrant atmosphere of the parades is driven by firecrackers, dance performances, and traditional music.

In the dawn of Nyepi, the island transforms into a serene paradise. The streets are deserted, and even Ngurah Rai International Airport suspends operations; it is one of the few occasions when an international airport shuts down. The quiet activities that are recommended for travellers include reading, meditation, and just soaking in the serenity of their surroundings.

One of the most defining characteristics of Nyepi is the "Catur Brata Penyepian " or Four Nyepi Prohibitions. Some of the restrictions that are observed by both locals and tourists are Amati Geni (no fire or light), Amati Karya (no work), Amati Lelungan (no travelling), and Amati Lelanguan (no delight or pleasure). These limitations are intended to help individuals connect with their spiritual selves and bring harmony back to the island.

Visitors have a special opportunity in Nyepi to completely immerse themselves in Balinese culture and discover more about the way of life there. Many hotels and resorts offer special packages and activities during Nyepi, including yoga retreats, meditation classes, and traditional Balinese entertainment. These features enable visitors to stay in luxury and comfort while still getting a real sense of Nyepi.

In conclusion, Nyepi is a very extraordinary festival that gives tourists to Bali a chance of a lifetime. It provides a thorough insight of Balinese culture, spirituality, and reflection. By participating in the rituals and keeping the day peaceful while learning more about the island's traditions, visitors may rejuvenate their own mind, body, and soul. Nyepi, a really unique event, showcases the beauty and wealth of Bali's traditional past.

## *Bali Spirit Festival*

If you are thinking of visiting Bali, you should not miss the Bali Spirit Festival. For travellers seeking a unique and soul-enriching holiday, this biennial celebration of music, dancing, yoga, and spirituality—which is considered as one of Southeast Asia's most exciting and transformative festivals—is a must-experience.

The annual Bali Spirit Festival is held in Ubud, Bali's cultural hub, and it attracts travellers from all over the world. The festival offers a broad range of activities that showcase the island's rich cultural history. The festival offers a fully immersive experience in the local arts scene, including everything from international music concerts to traditional Balinese dance and music acts.

One of the festival's main attractions is its extensive program of yoga and meditation lectures. Here, well-known spiritual leaders and yoga teachers from across the globe gather to share their wisdom and guide attendees on a journey of self-discovery and personal growth. Whether you're a seasoned yogi or just starting, this is a terrific opportunity to deepen your practice or give these practices a try for the first time. There are courses and seminars for every skill level.

Along with yoga and meditation, the Bali Spirit Festival offers a number of different health-related activities. There are workshops offered on ecstatic dance, breathwork, sound therapy, and many other subjects. These sessions provide you the chance to connect in a kind and supportive way with your body, mind, and spirit. It's a fantastic opportunity to revitalise and find equilibrium in Bali's serene and breathtaking surroundings.

The festival features a lovely marketplace with works by local artists and eco-friendly products in addition to the seminars and lectures. You may come across a wide selection of one-of-a-kind and eco-friendly souvenirs to bring home, ranging from handmade crafts to organic fashion and wellness products. Investigating the neighbourhood market might help you appreciate Balinese craftsmanship and give back to the community.

Along with individual experiences, the Bali Spirit Festival fosters a sense of community and connection. The festival provides a range of interactive and social events that encourage participants to socialise, exchange ideas, and appreciate diversity. Whether it is via group meals, panel discussions, or energetic musical performances, the event as a whole emits a spirit of celebration and unity.

Aside from the festival itself, Bali offers tourists a wide range of sites and activities. The island offers a variety of attractions, including lush rice terraces, ancient temples, stunning beaches, and a vibrant nightlife. You may take a day trip to one of the lovely nearby islands, discover Ubud's natural beauty, or visit the famed Monkey Forest after immersing yourself in the Bali Spirit Festival.

If you want to attend the Bali Spirit Festival, it is advisable to make your travel and housing arrangements in advance. Due to the enormous number of attendees at the event, there may not be much availability. Many people choose nearby homestays or eco-friendly resorts to thoroughly experience the local culture and enjoy a pleasant stay close to the festival location.

In conclusion, the Bali Spirit Festival is a transformative occasion that offers guests a unique blend of art, culture, health, and spirituality. If you want to grow personally, see another culture, or simply have an interesting and memorable vacation, this festival is the ideal destination. So mark your calendars and get ready for a soul-enriching trip to the alluring island of Bali.

## Ubud Food Festival

The Ubud Food Festival should be at the top of everyone's list of must-attend Bali events. This biennial event in the lovely town of Ubud honours Indonesia's rich and diverse culinary tradition while showcasing the prowess of both local and international chefs, restaurateurs, and food connoisseurs. The Ubud Food Festival's vibrant ambiance, mouth watering flavours, and fun activities make for a really unforgettable culinary experience.

One of the highlights of the Ubud Food Festival is the wide array of food booths and vendors serving up delicious Indonesian specialities. Every palate may be satisfied by a variety of foods, from traditional street food to contemporary fusion dishes. Tourists may sample regional dishes including nasi goreng (fried rice), sate (grilled skewers), and gado-gado (vegetable salad with peanut sauce). The occasion also offers regional specialties from Indonesia, allowing attendees to experience the many cuisines of the archipelago.

The Ubud Food Festival also provides cooking courses and seminars where visitors may hear prominent chefs divulge the secrets of Indonesian cuisine. These interactive sessions provide a unique opportunity to experience preparing regional foods using local ingredients and cooking techniques. Whether you are a seasoned chef or a kitchen beginner, these seminars are a terrific chance to improve your culinary skills and prepare some delicious recipes.

Along with the food, the festival offers a wide range of cultural events and entertainment, which improve the whole experience. Visitors may participate in food-related panel discussions, see traditional dance and music performances, and explore the vibrant art scene in Ubud. In addition to encouraging sustainability and ethical eating habits, the festival places a strong emphasis on assisting local farmers and artisans. It's an excellent resource for discovering how sustainability, culture, and gastronomy interact in Bali and worldwide.

In addition to savouring delectable food, the Ubud Food Festival provides an opportunity to socialise with other like-minded travellers and food enthusiasts from across the world. The festival attracts a diverse group of locals and visitors from all over the globe, generating a lively and hospitable atmosphere. Whether you're dining at a communal table, chatting with chefs during a cooking demonstration, or swapping stories with other food aficionados, the Ubud Food Festival is a place of warmth, camaraderie, and culinary exploration.

If you're attending the Ubud Food event, it's imperative to make your hotel reservations in advance since the town is quite busy during the event. Due to the wide range of hotel options in Ubud, from costly guesthouses to opulent resorts, any traveller may find a place that meets their needs. It's also a good idea to check the festival schedule in advance since there are often ticketed events and popular sessions that need to be booked in advance.

In conclusion, foodies and cultural aficionados travelling to Bali shouldn't miss the Ubud Food Festival. Due to its tantalising array of flavours and engaging culinary experiences, this festival promises to excite and delight your taste buds while also educating you about Indonesia's extensive culinary heritage. So get your hunger ready and get ready for the Ubud Food Festival's unique gastronomic trip.

## *Bali Arts Festival*

The magnificent Bali Arts Festival, which is held each year in Denpasar, the provincial capital, showcases the island's many artistic traditions. Visitors visiting Bali have the opportunity to meet the locals, take in dazzling performances, and learn about the artistic richness of this seductive island by attending the Bali Arts Festival.

The Bali Arts Festival, a month-long festival that takes place from June through July, attracts visitors and artists from all over the world. The festival offers a platform for local artists to showcase their prowess and maintain Bali's unique artistic tradition. Through a range of performances, such as traditional music, dance, puppetry, and theatre, it gives a glimpse of the island's various artistic traditions.

A grand opening ceremony including a colourful parade of participants from several Bali districts kicks off the festival. Both locals and tourists are mesmerised by the artistically stunning performance that features traditional clothing, intricate masks, and well-made accessories. Daily performances will be held at the Taman Werdhi Budaya Arts Center during the month-long celebration that follows the inauguration ceremony.

The Bali Arts Festival offers a wide range of cultural performances for guests to enjoy. Traditional Balinese dance forms like the Legong, Barong, and Kecak are performed; each tells a distinct story with lovely motions and rhyming music. The dances are backed by gamelan orchestras, which are composed of traditional percussion instruments and transport spectators to another era and location.

The occasion features not only dancing and music but also exquisite workmanship from Bali. As craftsmen display their skills in batik creation, painting, and wood carving, visitors may see the tedious process that goes into creating these lovely goods. Visitors may connect with the artists and learn about their methods in addition to purchasing handcrafted items as unique souvenirs.

One of the highlights of the Bali Arts Festival is the enormous art market, where visitors may peruse a large selection of handicrafts, textiles, and traditional artworks. The market is a treasure trove of unique items and a great location to buy authentic Balinese goods directly from the makers.

In addition to performances and exhibitions, the festival offers visitors the ability to actively engage in Bali's artistic legacy via workshops, lectures, and competitions. Visitors may enrol in dance sessions, take traditional instrument lessons from experienced local artists, or try their hand at painting.

The chance to witness the island's rich cultural past as well as get a deeper understanding of Bali's spirituality and way of life is provided by attending the Bali Arts Festival. The occasion exemplifies the Balinese idea of "Tri Hita Karana," which emphasises the harmony between humans, nature, and the spiritual realm.

For anyone seeking a fully immersive cultural experience, the Bali Arts Festival is a must-attend event. Tourists may see the rich traditions that have shaped the island's character and get a unique glimpse into Bali's personality. The Bali Arts Festival, which features breathtaking performances, exquisite craftsmanship, and friendly Balinese hospitality, is a wonderful journey into the heart of this captivating island's artistic heritage.

# Chapter 12. Practical Information

## *Currency and Money Exchange*

Understanding the local currency and the many options for money conversion is essential for a trouble-free financial trip to Bali. Here are some ideas to keep in mind:

Bali's official currency is the Indonesian Rupiah (IDR). It is a good idea to familiarise yourself with the currency and its denominations before your trip. The notes come in a variety of denominations, including 1,000, 2,000, 5,000, 10,000, 20,000, 50,000, and 100,000 Rupiah. Coins are still utilised, although they're generally used for little things.

Money Exchange: There are several options for exchanging currencies in Bali. You may exchange your currency at authorised banks, lodging establishments, or money changers. Although they might be convenient, hotels can have higher expenses and poor currency rates. Banks and reputable money changers often provide better exchange rates. Look for authorised money changers with transparent exchange rates shown on their counters to prevent becoming a victim of scam.

Exchange rates: Since exchange rates may fluctuate daily, it's crucial to keep track of them and compare them before making any purchases. Utilise reliable sources to check the current rates, such as reputable money exchange websites or financial programs. It's recommended to convert a little amount at the airport since rates there are often poorer; wait until you reach your hotel or a reputable money changer to receive better rates.

Despite the ease with which cash is accepted in Bali, it is always a good idea to carry some local currency. Many tiny enterprises, local markets, and street vendors may only take cash. However, larger stores, upscale restaurants, and luxury hotels often accept credit cards. Inform your bank in advance about your intended trip to avoid any issues with your cards being suspended due to dodgy activity.

ATMs: You can easily find ATMs all around Bali, especially in popular tourist areas. Even while using an ATM to get local currency is often a convenient alternative, certain ATMs may levy a withdrawal fee. Check with your bank to see if there are any limits or costs associated with using your card abroad. It is recommended to only use ATMs located in reputable banks and to avoid freestanding machines in less populated areas in order to limit the risk of card skimming.

Consider installing a trustworthy app for your smartphone before your trip to exchange currencies. These tools allow you to quickly calculate prices and get a deeper grasp of the local currency. Some apps can still run even if you don't have an internet connection.

Overall, you can ensure that your trip's finances go well by having local currency on hand and being informed of your options for converting money in Bali. By being familiar with the Indonesian Rupiah, researching conversion rates, and using trustworthy money changers or ATMs, you can make the most of your trip to this beautiful island without having to worry about money. Enjoy your stay in Bali and your journey!

## Communication and Internet Access

Anyone considering visiting this stunning island needs reliable communication and internet access so they can stay in contact, navigate the foreign surroundings, and take full advantage of their holiday.

There are several communication options available to visitors visiting Bali. The most common and useful method is to use a mobile phone. Tourists from other nations have two options: turning on international roaming on their own cell devices, or choosing local SIM cards. In Bali, prepaid SIM cards from various service providers are freely accessible at airports, convenience shops, and mobile phone retailers. These SIM cards come with data packages that provide customers access to the internet and affordable local and international calling.

Additionally, Bali has a robust communications infrastructure, and the majority of tourist sites often have consistent mobile coverage. However, if you plan to go to more remote or rural areas of the island, be aware that the signal strength may fluctuate and may be weaker in certain places.

In addition to mobile communication, Bali offers visitors a range of internet connection options. Most resorts, hotels, and inns provide free Wi-Fi to its patrons. This allows visitors to stay in contact, check their emails, and browse the web without paying additional expenses. These services often provide sufficient internet speeds for doing simple tasks, however real speeds may vary depending on the region and the number of users connecting to the network.

For those who want a more stable and speedy internet connection, Bali has a ton of internet cafes and co-working spaces. These locations provide pleasant work spaces, high-speed internet connection, and additional amenities like printing and scanning. They will be highly useful for digital nomads, remote workers, and anybody else who needs to do business while on the road.

Using mobile data is an extra way to access the internet in Bali. As mentioned earlier, tourists may purchase local SIM cards with data packages so they can use their mobile devices to access the internet. This option is quite useful for those who prefer to stay in touch while travelling and have a stable internet connection wherever they go on the island.

Bali offers a variety of options for communication and internet access, however connectivity may sometimes be limited or interrupted. Occasionally, network maintenance, power outages, and natural disasters may have an impact on communication services. Travellers should be prepared for such situations and have backup plans, such as offline maps or guidebooks, in order to navigate and communicate during such times.

In conclusion, travellers to Bali may often rely on and access reliable communication and internet connection. There are several methods to stay connected, including free Wi-Fi in hotels and specialist internet cafés, mobile connection using local SIM cards, and more. Travellers should have backup plans in case of disruptions and be mindful of potential fluctuations in signal quality, particularly in remote areas. By keeping these things in mind, visitors to Bali may benefit from a relaxing holiday while being connected to the outside world.

## Local Customs and Etiquette

For a gracious and enjoyable journey, tourists visiting Bali must familiarise themselves with local customs and etiquette. Here are some crucial factors to remember:

1. Courtesy and Politeness: Balinese people are renowned for their friendliness and kindness. When addressing a local person as "Sembah," it is customary to smile and bow gently. Handshakes are also acceptable in more formal circumstances. Remember to use your right hand as the left is considered to be filthy. Balinese people enjoy simple local greetings like "Om Swastiastu" (Hello) and "Suksma" (Thank you).

2. Clothes: Although Bali is known for its carefree beach lifestyle, it is nevertheless advisable to dress modestly, especially when

visiting temples or rural areas. Both men and women should cover their shoulders and wear long pants or skirts while visiting holy sites. Outside of popular tourist areas, wearing skimpy clothing in public is often frowned upon. You may demonstrate that you respect local customs and standards by how you dress.

3. Etiquette at Temples: Visiting Bali's famous temples, which are noted for their exquisite architecture, is a must-do excursion. Don't forget to wear a sarong, a traditional cloth, around your waist as a sign of respect. Always be respectful and silent while visiting temples since they are places of prayer. Never place your foot near an offering or point it toward a shrine. Take the indigenous' example and follow their lead without meddling if you're at a ceremony.

4. Balinese Offerings: Each day, elegant tiny offerings known as "canang sari" are left at homes, businesses, and temples around Bali. These donations are a show of gratitude and adoration. You shouldn't kick or trample on them

since they are treasured. If you have a chance to encounter one, carefully avoid it.

5. Respect for Elders: In Balinese culture, it's crucial to treat elders with respect. Talk to the elderly people in the region in a kind and respectful manner. They are used to respectful bows during greetings and civil discourse. Be mindful of your tone and body language to convey respect.

6. Public Conduct: Given that Bali is a mostly Hindu island, certain actions could be seen adversely. Avoid making public displays of affection since they are frowned upon, especially in rural areas. By keeping your lips shut and controlling your anger, you may avoid being impolite and disruptive. You may respect local traditions and customs by acclimating to the peaceful and enjoyable way of life.

7. Cultural Sensitivity: It's important to respect regional traditions and beliefs since Bali has a rich cultural heritage. Get people's permission

before taking their photo, especially at religious events. Touching someone's head is prohibited since it is valued. When you pay someone a visit at their house, it's customary to bring a gift of appreciation like fruit or flowers.

8. Tipping is not necessary but appreciated in Bali. It is customary to leave a little gratuity as a token of gratitude when a transportation, restaurant, or hotel offers exceptional service. Giving them some money in appreciation for their labour might go a long way.

By following certain local customs and etiquette, you will respect Balinese culture and enhance your own vacation experience. If you accept Bali's beauty with an open mind and heart, the friendly natives will welcome you with love and generosity.

## Useful Phrases

If you're planning a trip to the beautiful island of Bali, it's always handy to have some useful phrases in your repertoire to help you navigate your way around, interact with locals, and make the most of your experience worthwhile. Some common phrases you can learn are :

1. Selamat pagi/siang/malam - Good morning/afternoon/evening.
2. Terima kasih - Thank you.
3. Tolong - Please.
4. Apa kabar? - How are you?
5. Saya baik-baik saja - I'm fine.
6. Apa nama Anda? - What is your name?
7. Nama saya ___ - My name is ___ .
8. Di mana toilet? - Where is the toilet?
9. Tidak apa-apa - It's okay.
10. Ya - Yes.
11. Tidak - No.

12. Permisi - Excuse me.

13. Maaf - Sorry.

14. Berapa harganya? - How much is it?

15. Boleh saya melihat-lihat? - Can I have a look around?

16. Bisakah Anda membantu saya? - Can you help me?

17. Saya tidak mengerti - I don't understand.

18. Di mana alamat ___? - Where is the address ___?

19. Tolong antar saya ke ___ - Please take me to ___.

20. Ada WiFi di sini? - Is there WiFi here?

21. Tolong berbicara lebih lambat - Please speak slower.

22. Ada yang bisa saya bantu? - Can I help you with something?

23. Berapa lama perjalanan ini? - How long does this journey take?

24. Ini enak sekali! - This is delicious!

25. Ada rekomendasi restoran yang bagus? - Do you have any recommendations for good restaurants?

26. Bisa pesan taksi untuk saya? - Can you order a taxi for me?

27. Di mana saya bisa tukar uang? - Where can I exchange money?

28. Saya ingin memesan meja untuk dua orang - I would like to book a table for two people.

29. Ada yang bisa saya lakukan di sekitar sini? - Is there anything to do around here?

30. Ada toko suvenir di dekat sini? - Is there a souvenir shop nearby?

31. Tolong tulis ini untuk saya - Please write this down for me.

32. Bisakah Anda berbicara bahasa Inggris? - Can you speak English?

33. Tolong panggilkan ambulans - Please call an ambulance.

34. Saya kehilangan dompet saya - I lost my wallet.

35. Saya butuh bantuan polisi - I need help from the police.

36. Tolong tunggu sebentar - Please wait a moment.

37. Bisakah Anda mengulanginya? - Can you repeat that?

38. Tolong isi ulang minuman saya - Please refill my drink.

39. Di mana saya bisa mendapatkan bantuan medis? - Where can I get medical assistance?

40. Apakah ini tawar? - Is this negotiable?

41. Tolong jangan tinggalkan saya sendirian - Please don't leave me alone.

42. Saya kehausan - I'm thirsty.

43. Tolong buka jendela - Please open the window.

44. Tolong tutup pintu - Please close the door.

45. Tolong bawa saya ke bandara - Please take me to the airport.

46. Tolong jaga barang-barang saya - Please

## Emergency Contacts

Before departing on a trip, particularly one to Bali, it's important to be prepared for any emergency or unforeseen circumstances. If you have the right emergency contacts, you may have confidence that you will get assistance as soon as you need it. Keep in mind these figures when you go to Bali:

1. Local Emergency Services: In the event of a medical emergency, an accident, or any other urgent situation, it is crucial to know the local emergency phone numbers. The main emergency number in Bali is 112, which will connect you to the local police, fire department, or ambulance service. Ensure that you always have access to this number.

2. Hospitals and Clinics: Learn about the nearest hospitals and clinics to your accommodation. A few well-known hospitals in Bali include Kasih Ibu Hospital in Ubud, Sanglah General Hospital in Denpasar, and BIMC Hospital in Kuta. Make sure you have access to their contact information at all times.

3. Embassy or Consulate: It is a good idea to register with the embassy or consulate of your home country before travelling to Bali. They may provide you assistance, encouragement, and

crucial information when you need it. Learn how to get in touch with your embassy or consulate and keep the details securely.

4. Travel Insurance Provider: Make sure you have quick access to the company's contact details if you have travel insurance. If you experience a medical emergency while travelling or if you are having any other issues, get in touch with your insurance company as soon as you can for guidance and support.

5. Local Police: While you may contact the local police by dialling emergency services (112), knowing the direct phone number of the nearest police station in the area where you are staying may be helpful. They might assist you with issues like lost or stolen goods, stolen passports, and other legal issues that could arise while you're travelling.

6. If you used a tour operator to arrange your trip or are staying at a certain hotel, have the company's contact details close to hand. They

might be a valuable resource if you have any inquiries or want assistance while travelling.

7. Travel agency: Keep their contact information handy if you utilise a travel agency to plan your trip to Bali. They can help you and guide you through everything that unexpectedly arises while you're travelling.

8. Local Transport Services: If you plan to use any local transportation services, such taxis or ride-hailing apps, it's a good idea to save the contact details of those services on your phone. This will make it easier for you to get in touch with them if you ever run into issues with your transportation.

Do not forget to keep these emergency phone numbers on your phone, a physical notepad, and an online note-taking application. Give a trustworthy friend or family back home a copy of these details so they can assist you if needed.

Although Bali is a generally safe place, knowing the right emergency contacts may provide you a sense of security and ensure that you get assistance right away if any unanticipated events arise while you're there.

# Chapter 13. Accommodation Options

## *Luxury Resorts and Villas*

Bali offers a range of luxurious resorts and villas that are ideal for the discerning traveller due to its stunning surroundings, vibrant culture, and kind hospitality. Whether you're looking for a romantic getaway, a family vacation, or a rejuvenating retreat, Bali's luxurious accommodations provide an unparalleled experience.

One of Bali's most remarkable attractions is the stunning scenery of its luxury resorts and villas. These homes, which are hidden away in the picturesque hills of the island or situated above stunning beaches, provide tranquil settings and breathtaking views. From the moment you arrive, you'll be greeted with smiles and service that goes above and beyond the call of duty.

Luxury resorts in Bali are highly recognized for their first-rate amenities and services. You may indulge in opulent spa treatments, cool down in pools with breathtaking views, or participate in a range of outdoor activities including yoga, surfing, and golf. Many resorts also feature private beaches where you may relax in peace and enjoy the beautiful waves of the Indian Ocean.

For those seeking even more solitude and seclusion, Bali's opulent villas provide an exceptional experience. Large living areas, private pools, and dedicated staff in these opulent residences provide a home-away-from-home feel. Whether you choose a beachfront villa, a cliffside retreat, or a secluded jungle hideaway, you'll have the chance to unwind and take in Bali's natural beauty at your own speed.

Bali's luxurious resorts and villas provide sumptuous accommodations as well as a diverse culinary scene. Many resorts provide a range of dining options, from upscale restaurants to relaxed seaside cafés. You may sample a variety of international cuisines, including authentic Balinese dishes prepared by outstanding cooks using locally sourced ingredients. When the best food, first-rate ambiance, and attentive service are combined, a fantastic dining experience is created.

Bali's luxurious housing alternatives provide opportunities to explore and get fully immersed in the local culture. Participate in ancient ceremonies, learn traditional crafts, or sign up for a cooking lesson to learn the secrets of Balinese cuisine. Private trips to well-known locations like Tanah Lot Temple, the lush rice terraces of Ubud, or the venerated Mount Batur may be arranged via the hotel concierge services. To truly appreciate the island's flourishing cultural scene, visit local art galleries or attend traditional dance performances.

The variety of magnificent resorts and villas in Bali has something to offer every traveller. Whether you're searching for adventure, leisure, or a mix of the two, you may choose a house that meets your requirements. The island's mild climate, stunning natural beauty, and rich cultural history combine to make it the ideal setting for a luxurious vacation.

In conclusion, Bali's lavish resorts and villas are unmatched for travellers looking for a luxurious hideaway. With their magnificent locations, top-notch amenities, and kind service, these establishments provide a haven of luxury and calm. Whether you wish to explore the island's natural wonders, immerse yourself in Balinese culture, or just unwind by the pool, Bali's luxurious accommodations provide an outstanding journey that will leave you with cherished memories for a lifetime.

## Budget Hotels and Guesthouses

Whether you're a backpacker, a thrifty traveller, or looking for a more authentic experience, Bali offers a choice of affordable housing options, including low-cost hotels and guesthouses. These companies provide comfortable lodging at reasonable prices, allowing guests to make the most of their vacation without going over their travel budget.

The budget hotels and guesthouses in Bali provide a variety of amenities and services, ensuring a pleasant stay without breaking the bank. They may not be as lavish as luxury resorts, but they more than make up for it with their friendly atmosphere, endearing local flair, and affordable costs. These accommodations are particularly popular among alone travellers, backpackers, and those who wish to spend more money exploring the island's attractions and activities.

One advantage is the thoughtful positioning of inexpensive hotels and guesthouses. The fact that they are often found in well-known tourist areas like Kuta, Seminyak, Ubud, and Canggu makes it straightforward to get to Bali's renowned beaches, historical sites, and vibrant nightlife. Whether you're seeking for a relaxing beach holiday, a spiritual retreat in the picturesque surroundings of Ubud, or an action-packed island tour, you may find affordable accomodation close to your chosen spots.

In Bali, inexpensive hotels and guesthouses provide convenience and cleanliness without compromising their affordable rates. Many of these places provide spotless rooms with typical amenities like air conditioning, comfortable beds, private restrooms, and WiFi. Some even provide supplemental services like restaurants, swimming pools, and bike rentals to make your stay even more convenient and enjoyable.

The kind and welcoming staff of Bali's budget hotels and guesthouses is well known. Genuine local hospitality ensures that guests are made to feel at home throughout their stay. The staff members often have a wealth of knowledge about the island and may provide wise counsel on neighbouring activities, means of transportation, and dining options. Their assistance might greatly enhance your vacation to Bali by pointing you to hidden gems and less visited areas.

Another benefit of choosing economical accommodation in Bali is the opportunity to completely experience local culture. You could get an intimate insight of the island's many cultures and customs since many guesthouses are owned and operated by Balinese families. These locations, with their intricate Balinese architecture, traditional decor, and authentic local cuisine, provide a particular cultural experience that you won't find in larger, more commercialised hotels.

Bali's inexpensive hotels and guesthouses are far less costly than high-end resorts. Prices vary depending on the location, amenities, and time of year, although they are often within reach of regular vacationers. Because Bali is so easily accessible, visitors may spend their money on more fun pursuits like surfing, snorkelling, or hiking as well as on exploring the island's breathtaking natural surroundings and exquisite local cuisine.

In conclusion, travellers seeking affordable and comfortable accomodation have several options among Bali's budget hotels and guesthouses. They provide a welcoming atmosphere, useful settings, and a chance to interact directly with the local culture. Due to their reasonable prices and basic amenities, these locations allow visitors to get the most out of their time in Bali without going over budget. If you're planning a trip to Bali and want to stretch your travel budget while still enjoying all the island has to offer, think about staying in one of the many low-cost hotels or guesthouses the island has to offer.

## *Homestays and Airbnb*

One of the most important decisions you'll make while planning a trip to Bali is picking the right hotel. Bali has become a sought-after travel destination for travellers from all over the world because of its stunning surroundings, vibrant culture, and friendly locals. Two excellent options for housing in Bali are homestays and Airbnb rentals, each of which provides unique experiences and the chance to truly experience the local way of life.

Balinese families often offer their homes for homestays to give tourists a glimpse into native life. Visitors may encourage cultural exchange and create lifelong experiences by connecting with the people individually during their visit. Balinese families are known for their warmth and hospitality; they go out of their way to make tourists feel welcome.

One of the biggest advantages of picking a homestay is the opportunity to experience Balinese culture firsthand. Many homestays provide traditional cooking classes where guests may learn how to prepare traditional Balinese food using local ingredients and time-honoured techniques. You also have the choice to participate in traditional ceremonies or learn conventional skills like batik painting or wood carving. These interactions go above and beyond what is typical for visitors and provide a deeper understanding of Balinese culture.

Homestays are often situated in serene and lovely settings, hidden amid picturesque villages or surrounded by green rice terraces. It is hard to replicate in crowded tourist locations the tranquil atmosphere that is produced by waking up to the sound of roosters crowing and breathing in the fresh country air. Tourists may relax and reenergize away from the bustle of city life in the tranquil setting of homestays.

In contrast, Bali's Airbnb rentals provide a selection of hotel options that may suit a range of preferences and budgets. No matter if you're looking for a cosy villa in Ubud, a beachfront property in Seminyak, or a luxurious hideaway in Nusa Dua, you may find a number of Airbnb listings that suit your interests. These rentals provide visitors a sense of solitude and flexibility that allows them to organise their own schedules and make themselves at home while travelling.

Modern comforts like private pools, fully equipped kitchens, and spacious living areas are often offered in Airbnb rentals to make sure guests have a good time. Many hosts also provide their visitors recommendations, leading them to new tourism attractions like undiscovered beaches and undiscovered landmarks. Thanks to Airbnb's ease and adaptability, you can tailor your lodgings to suit your particular requirements whether you're travelling alone, in a couple, or with a group of friends.

Additionally, both Airbnb rentals and homestays provide excellent value for the money. These options nonetheless provide comfort and unique experiences while often being more affordable than traditional hotels and resorts. By choosing a homestay or Airbnb lodging, tourists may stretch their budget and save additional cash to spend on seeing Bali's many attractions, enjoying local cuisine, or participating in exhilarating outdoor activities.

Finally, while planning travel arrangements to Bali, consider the unique experiences and benefits that homestays and Airbnb rentals have to offer. Whether you choose for an Airbnb rental for privacy and independence or a homestay to really experience Balinese culture, both options provide a terrific opportunity to truly make your vacation to Bali one-of-a-kind. To assure a delightful vacation throughout the attractive island of Bali, choose the hotel that best suits your needs and accept the kindness of the Balinese people.

# Chapter 14. Sustainable Tourism in Bali

## *Eco-friendly Practices*

Eco-friendly activities are of the utmost importance to tourists to Bali, a popular tourist destination known for its stunning landscapes, extensive cultural past, and unique biodiversity. In view of the rising concern for environmental sustainability, travellers must adopt eco-friendly habits and promote responsible tourism. By including these activities into their holiday plans, tourists can help protect Bali's natural beauty and support the local economy. Visitors to Bali might benefit by adhering to these eco-friendly rules.

Accommodation selection that is sustainable should be prioritised. Search for eco-friendly hotels that give waste reduction, water conservation, and energy management first priority. These companies often recycle, utilise sustainable energy sources, and promote water conservation among clients by putting in place initiatives like towel and linen reuse.

Travellers may also have a significant impact on the transportation sector. Use walking or cycling as an ecologically responsible means of transportation wherever possible, especially when travelling small distances. Bali is the ideal location to explore on foot or by bicycle due to its tiny size and stunning surroundings. Using public transportation like buses or shuttles may be more ecologically beneficial than operating a private vehicle. If you must rent a vehicle, consider selecting an electric or hybrid model.

To reduce plastic waste, bring a reusable water bottle and fill it up at one of the numerous locations that provide filtered water stations. Use cans or glass containers instead of single-use plastic bottles while you're drinking. Plastic pollution in Bali has increased, and responsible visitors may help to solve this issue by forgoing the use of single-use plastics.

The local wildlife and nature must be respected. Be careful not to damage or destroy coral reefs when snorkelling or scuba diving since they are sensitive ecosystems. To protect the local flora, take care to step lightly and stick to the routes while hiking in the wilderness. Avoid feeding or interacting with wild animals since doing so might disrupt their natural behaviour and be detrimental to their long-term wellbeing.

Two strategies to support nearby businesses and communities are to buy locally made items and dine at neighbourhood restaurants. This advances both the cultural experience and the economic growth of the area. Look for souvenirs and crafts manufactured from sustainable materials like bamboo or recycled materials rather than products derived from non-renewable resources or endangered animals.

Take part in community initiatives or volunteer endeavours that have an emphasis on environmental preservation. Several organisations in Bali hold educational lectures, reforestation campaigns, and beach clean-ups to promote awareness of sustainable practices. By actively participating in these activities, tourists may have a positive impact and assist in the preservation of Bali's natural resources.

Lastly, educate yourself on Bali's environmental initiatives and challenges. Learn about the island's unique ecosystems, including its forests, mangroves, and rice terraces, and understand the importance of maintaining them. Engage in respectful and responsible tourism by keeping in mind local customs and traditions and adhering to any restrictions set by the authorities of the destination.

In conclusion, eco-friendly conduct among tourists to Bali is essential to preserving the island's natural beauty and fostering sustainable tourism. By choosing eco-friendly lodgings, taking part in community projects, reducing plastic waste, respecting nature and wildlife, using eco-friendly transportation, and choosing sustainable accommodations, tourists can ensure that future generations can continue to enjoy Bali's wonders. Let's all strive to travel sensibly and protect Bali's beauty.

## *Responsible Travel Tips*

The impact of their acts on the local environment, culture, and communities should be considered by tourists. Responsible travel practices should provide a positive and sustainable experience for guests and the local population in addition to conserving Bali's natural beauty. Before visiting Bali, keep the following in mind to travel safely:

1. Respect Local Culture: Bali has a rich and diverse cultural past. It is important to respect local traditions, customs, and religious beliefs. Dress modestly and use care while entering temples and other religious buildings to prevent upsetting anybody. Spend some time learning about Balinese customs and etiquette before

your trip to make sure you can communicate respectfully with the people.

2. Support Local Businesses: One of the best ways to improve your community is by shopping locally. Stay at locally owned hotels, restaurants, and shops rather than picking international franchises. Buying locally made goods and souvenirs supports regional artisans and keeps traditional craftsmanship alive.

3. Reduce Plastic Waste: Bali has experienced environmental issues as a result of plastic waste. To help with the solution, cut down on your usage of plastic. Bring a refillable water bottle that you can use at water stations rather than buying single-use plastic bottles. Refusing to use plastic bags means bringing your own reusable shopping bag. Participate in beach cleaning initiatives to keep Bali's beaches clean.

4. Conserve Water and Energy: Bali's water resources are few. By taking shorter showers and turning off the water while the faucet is not in

use, you may reduce the amount of water you consume. The same applies to keeping your accommodation's lights, air conditioning, and other electrical devices on while you're gone. When possible, replace air conditioning with natural ventilation.

5. Choose Eco-Friendly Activities: While visiting Bali, visitors may engage in a variety of eco-friendly and sustainable activities. Participate in eco-friendly pursuits like snorkelling and diving with trustworthy operators that prioritise marine preservation. By hiking and bicycling, seeing organic farms, or engaging in sustainable tourism activities, you may discover Bali's natural beauty.

6. Respect the wildlife: Bali is home to a wide range of animals, including endangered species. Avoid going to events where animals are used as entertainment, such as elephant rides or dolphin or monkey performances. For ethically sound contact with animals, choose animal sanctuaries or conservation programs.

7. Take Part in Responsible Outdoor Adventures: Trekking, hiking, and other outdoor activities are ideal in Bali's natural settings. To protect vulnerable ecosystems, only engage in these activities on designated paths and walkways. Animals in the wild should not be fed or bothered. You may be certain that you leave no trace by properly disposing of any trash.

8. Use Transportation Carefully: Bali sometimes has high traffic, especially in tourist hotspots. Try to travel as sustainably as you can by walking, riding, or using public transportation. If you opt to rent a scooter or a car, drive carefully and according to all local traffic regulations.

9. Involve Local Communities: Develop sincere and polite relationships with the locals. Learn a few basic words and phrases in Bahasa Indonesia, the local language, so that you can communicate and connect with the Balinese people. Participate in neighbourhood-focused

philanthropic volunteer activities, but make sure your commitment is true and sustained.

10. Leave No Trace: Bali should follow the last and most crucial ethical vacation tip. You may leave no trace of your stay by properly disposing of your trash, not leaving behind any litter, and maintaining environmental respect. When visiting cultural sites, hiking through the jungle, or exploring the beaches, always clean up after yourself and leave the area as you found it.

Encourage initiatives for sustainable tourism: Look for vacation companies and accommodations that support local conservation programs and use sustainable practices. Many organisations in Bali work to preserve the environment and cultural heritage. By choosing to support these initiatives, you may contribute to the long-term sustainability of Bali's tourism industry.

12. Educate Yourself: Before your vacation, take the time to read about Bali's history, culture, and

environmental problems. Discover ethical travel strategies and become aware of the issues the island is experiencing. If you have this knowledge, you'll be able to make wiser decisions and travel with more responsibility.

13. Conserve Water: Water is scarce in Bali, particularly during the dry season. Shorten your showers and avoid leaving the water running continuously. Consider reserving accommodations that include water-saving amenities like low-flow toilets and drought-tolerant landscaping.

14. Respect Marine Life: Due to Bali's abundant marine biodiversity, snorkelling and diving are popular tourist activities. When engaging in these activities, be mindful of the delicate marine ecosystem. You should never stand on or touch coral reefs, and you should never remove marine life or shells from their natural habitat.

15. Participate in Community-Based tourism: By taking part in community-based tourism

initiatives, visitors may directly contribute to the development of the local economy. Consider visiting historic towns, attending cultural activities, or enrolling in local craft workshops. These tours provide visitors a true glimpse into Balinese culture while also assisting the local population in maintaining their way of life.

16. Reduce Your Carbon Footprint: Flying contributes to the greenhouse gas emissions that fuel climate change. Consider lowering your carbon footprint by supporting programs designed to reduce greenhouse gas emissions. The various organisations that provide carbon offset programs may be used to quantify and make up for your travel-related carbon footprints.

If you wish to interact with animals while travelling, educate yourself on animal welfare. Avoid engaging in activities that include riding, utilising animals in performances, or mistreating them. Opt instead for reputable wildlife refuges that promote conservation, rescue, and rehabilitation initiatives.

18. Promote careful waste management in Bali since there is a lot of trash there. Put your trash in the proper bins to show that you are responsible for it. If you live in a remote area without access to waste management services, you will need to carry your trash with you until you find a convenient place to dispose of it.

19. Respect the Environment: Bali's breathtaking natural surroundings are one of its main attractions. Avoid harming plants, picking flowers, or disturbing animals to show respect for the environment. In protected places, follow any regulations or laws, remain on designated trails, and tidy up after yourself.

20. Spread the Word: Share your stories of responsible travel with others. Encourage friends, relatives, and other travellers to use safe travel practices while visiting Bali or any other destination. By encouraging responsible tourism

and raising knowledge of its advantages, we can all contribute to a more sustainable future for Bali and the whole world.

Never forget that responsible travel entails making choices that maximise beneficial benefits and limit harmful ones. With the aid of these suggestions, you may have a lovely vacation to Bali while also doing good deeds for the locals, the environment, and the local communities.

## *Supporting Local Communities*

Despite the fact that the island's natural beauty and historic traditions attract many visitors, it's vital to remember that tourism may have both positive and negative consequences on neighbouring towns. Helping local communities should be the main concern for every visitor to Bali in order to ensure an ethical and environmentally friendly trip.

One of the most effective ways to support local communities is to choose housing options that have a positive influence. Instead of booking a chain hotel overseas, think about staying in a locally owned guesthouse, a homestay, or an eco-friendly resort. You immediately contribute to the local families' livelihoods and the upkeep of their cultural heritage by doing this. Consider organising excursions and activities offered by community organisations or regional tour operators who are knowledgeable about Bali culture and can deliver authentic experiences.

Another method to support the community economy is to purchase gifts and handcrafted products directly from local artisans and markets. Bali celebrates intricate wood carvings, textiles made in the region, and traditional artwork. Instead than buying mass-produced items from tourist shops, browse local markets and speak with artisans to learn about their work. Not only will you be able to bring home one-of-a-kind keepsakes that have special meaning for you, but you'll also be directly supporting artisans and preserving ancient techniques.

When dining out, responsible travellers should choose local eateries over franchises from other countries. Balinese cuisine is an intriguing fusion of flavours, and by dining at local establishments, you support individual businesses and the farmers who provide them with regional produce. Genuine Balinese cuisine may be enjoyed in a variety of settings, from humble warungs (local food sellers) to family-run restaurants, all while supporting the regional food industry.

Two more efficient methods to assist Bali's local communities are by volunteering and taking part in community-based initiatives. The major objectives of several organisations and projects are environmental preservation, education, and social welfare. Consider helping out at local schools, participating in beach clean-ups, or contributing to initiatives that promote women and marginalised groups. These interactions not only help you make a difference but also improve your knowledge of the problems and objectives of the neighbouring communities.

Respect for Balinese culture and traditions is necessary for tourism to be long-lasting. The majority of the people in Bali are Hindu, and the island is covered with temples and sacred locations. Visitors should dress modestly, cover their shoulders, and wear sarongs before entering these holy sites. Through polite and sensitive encounters with the local community, mutual understanding and respect are encouraged.

Last but not least, if you want to assist the locals in Bali, you need to consider how your actions could impact the environment. The island has to cope with difficulties including waste management and a lack of water. As a responsible traveller, lessen your use of plastic, pack a reusable water bottle, and engage in eco-friendly activities. You may support hotels and businesses that prioritise sustainability by using eco-friendly practices, recycling, and energy-saving measures.

In conclusion, giving back to Bali's local communities not only satisfies a moral obligation but also provides tourists with a rewarding and rich experience. By choosing locally owned accommodations, engaging with local artisans, dining at nearby eateries, volunteering, respecting cultural traditions, and practising environmental responsibility, tourists may contribute to the island's social and economic development. Let's adopt a responsible travel mindset and make sure that our trip to Bali has an impact that is beneficial and lasting on the locals of this attractive island.

# Chapter 15. Beyond Bali

## *Day Trips from Bali*

There are plenty of things to do and see in Bali itself, but it also makes a perfect base for exploring the adjacent islands and tourist destinations. Consider taking some exhilarating day excursions when planning a trip to Bali to discover more about Indonesia's natural splendours. Here are some fantastic options to think about:

1. Nusa Penida: Only a short boat ride from Bali, Nusa Penida is a must-see destination for nature lovers. The island has breathtaking cliffs, clear waters, and spotless white sand beaches. Don't miss the chance to visit Kelingking Beach, Broken Beach, and Angel's Billabong. It is highly recommended to go diving or snorkelling around Crystal Bay.

2. Gili Islands: A beach lover's paradise, the Gili Islands are situated off the northwest coast of Lombok. Three tiny islands, Gili Trawangan, Gili Meno, and Gili Air, are home to magnificent coral reefs, a healthy marine ecology, and a laid-back island vibe. Enjoy cycling among the islands, snorkelling, sunning, and Gili Trawangan's vibrant nightlife.

3. Mount Batur: In the northeast of Bali, there is an active volcano named Mount Batur. If you're ready for a challenge, consider a morning trek to the summit. The short hike will pay off with a stunning sunrise and panoramic views of the surroundings, including Lake Batur. After that, relax next to outdoor hot springs for a really rejuvenating experience.

4. Ubud and its Surroundings: Known as the cultural epicentre of Bali, Ubud is home to a broad range of attractions. Visit the famed Tegalalang Rice Terraces, the spectacular Ubud Monkey Forest, and get immersed in the world of traditional arts and crafts. Take advantage of

the chance to attend a health retreat at a famous resort in Ubud or see a traditional Balinese dance performance.

5. Sekumpul Waterfall: Sekumpul Waterfall, which is situated in the north of Bali, is often referred to as the most beautiful waterfall on the whole island. To reach there, one must travel through thick woods, cross streams, and climb steep steps. The effort is justified when you see the spectacular sight of multiple waterfalls rushing into a natural pool.

6. A day trip to the West Bali National Park, which is a protected area with a variety of ecosystems including coral reefs, mangrove forests, and rainforests, would be appealing to nature enthusiasts. Take a guided hike around the park, hunt for endangered bird species, or take a boat to Menjangan Island for diving and snorkelling of the highest calibre.

7. Tanah Lot Temple, one of Bali's most well-known landmarks, is located on the

southwest coast of the island. This ancient Hindu temple is perched on a rock formation and offers stunning views of the sun setting. Visit the local stores, stroll around the area, and eat delicious seafood at a restaurant on the shore.

These are just a few of the incredible day trips you can do from Bali. Each location offers a unique opportunity to experience Indonesia's natural beauty, cultural tradition, and adventurous spirit. Pack your bags, go outside of Bali, and build amazing memories as you explore the fascinating richness found close to this tropical refuge.

## Nearby Islands and Attractions

Despite Bali's abundance of attractions, the nearby islands provide even more opportunities for exploration and adventure. From peaceful retreats to spectacular water sports, the nearby islands offer a range of activities to complement a trip to Bali. Here are some nearby islands and attractions that visitors to Bali may want to consider visiting.

1. Nusa Penida, an island southeast of Bali, is well known for its untamed beauty and pristine beaches. Kelingking Beach's T-Rex-shaped bluff is a must-visit spot for panoramic views. Angel's Billabong, Broken Beach, and Crystal Bay are excellent places for divers and snorkelers to observe unusual natural formations.

2. Nusa Lembongan: This leisurely island hideaway is close to Bali via boat. Dream Beach and Mushroom Bay both have swimmable seas and are well-liked spots to sunbathe. Adventurers may engage in activities including snorkelling, diving, and surfing. Visitors visiting the neighbouring island of Nusa Ceningan, which is linked to Nusa Lembongan by the magnificent Yellow Bridge, may explore hidden coves and take advantage of the Blue Lagoon, which is renowned for its beauty.

3. Gili Islands: Off the northwest coast of Lombok, the Gili Islands are a tropical paradise. The largest of the three islands, Gili Trawangan, is home to breath-taking beaches and turquoise waters with a vibrant nightlife. Gili Air is famed for its tranquil atmosphere, while Gili Meno is ideal for honeymooners and those seeking seclusion. On the islands, cycling, diving, and snorkelling are popular pastimes.

4. Lombok: Although not a close neighbour to Bali, Lombok is nonetheless easily accessible by boat or plane. Hikers who conquer the challenging climb up Mount Rinjani, an active volcano, are rewarded with breathtaking views from the summit. Beautiful beaches like those in Kuta and Tanjung Aan are great for swimming and tanning. Lombok's traditional Sasak villages provide a glimpse into the island's way of life and culture.

5. Menjangan Island: To the northwest of Bali lies Menjangan Island, which is a part of West Bali National Park. This little island is a haven

for snorkelers and divers because of its stunning coral reefs, which are home to a variety of marine life. The clear waters allow for excellent eyesight, and encounters with sea turtles and colourful fish are common. There are numerous rare bird species to observe, and the island's lush woodlands may be explored.

6. Nusa Ceningan: The Yellow Bridge connects this serene island to Nusa Lembongan, and it is recognized for its breathtaking beauty. In the Blue Lagoon, which is renowned for its breathtaking blue waters, cliff jumping and swimming are additional well-liked pastimes. While Secret Beach provides a tranquil retreat, Mahana Point Cliff Jump offers thrill-seekers an adrenaline-pumping experience.

7. Nusa Dua: Located on the southern coast of Bali, Nusa Dua is well known for its luxurious hotels and exquisite beaches. The area offers a wide range of water sports, including banana boat tours, parasailing, and jet skiing. Visitors may also travel to the nearby Water Blow, where

enormous waves pound against the rocks and put on a spectacular show.

By allowing travellers to go outside of the main island, these nearby islands and locations provide a trip to Bali a new dimension. Each island offers unique opportunities for relaxation and adventure, from stunning beaches and risk-taking water sports to the diverse cultural experiences. Whether tourists are seeking action or peace and quiet, these nearby islands provide an incredible experience.

Made in United States
Troutdale, OR
07/08/2023